LET THE READER UNDERSTAND

Sean Goan

Let the Reader Understand

THE SUNDAY READINGS OF YEAR B

the columba press

First published in 2008 by
the columba press
55A Spruce Avenue, Stillorgan Industrial Park,
Blackrock, Co Dublin

Cover by Bill Bolger
Origination by The Columba Press
Printed in Ireland by ColourBooks Ltd, Dublin

ISBN 978 1 85607 630 2

Table of Contents

Foreword   6
Introduction   7

The Season of Advent   18

The Season of Christmas
    The Vigil Mass   26
    Midnight Mass   27
    The Dawn Mass   28
    Mass during the Day   29
    Feast of the Holy Family   30
    Second Sunday after Christmas   32

The Season of Lent   34
    Passion Sunday (Palm Sunday)   43

The Season of Easter
    Easter Sunday   45
    The Ascension of the Lord   55
    Pentecost Sunday   57

Feasts of the Lord in Ordinary Time
    Trinity Sunday   60
    The Body and Blood of Christ   61

Ordinary Time
    The Baptism of the Lord   64
    Sundays of the Year   65
    The Feast of Christ the Universal King   122

Foreword

This volume is the third and last in the series of fully revised and edited articles that appeared in the *Word* magazine between 1996 and 2002. I would like once again to express my gratitude to Fr Tom Cahill SVD and the Divine Word Missionaries for their help and support during the original project and also in bringing about this publication.

I wish to dedicate this volume to the team at the Orlagh Retreat Centre in Dublin. For the last ten years it has been my privilege and pleasure to work closely with John Byrne OSA, Dr Kieran O'Mahony OSA, Dr Bernadette Toal, Mary Kearney, Eilis O Malley and Dr Carmel McCarthy RSM. During that time the team has provided courses, workshops and retreats for people from all over Ireland and beyond. The Centre has been a haven of peace and a place of discovery for many. God grant that its work may continue long into the future.

Sean Goan

Introduction

Reading the New Testament

The three-year cycle for the Sunday readings puts before us passages from both the Old and New Testaments. Each week we hear one Old Testament text, followed by a Psalm and then followed by two from the New Testament. The reason for the emphasis on the New Testament is clear enough; here we find the early church witnessing to the good news of the life, death and resurrection of Jesus Christ our Lord. However, that does not mean that the New Testament makes for easy reading. Just like the Old, it too grew out of a context very different from our own. It was written in a language we do not know and mostly by Jews whose rich religious inheritance is not familiar to many Christians. Jesus himself was a Jew and made much use of the scriptures of his people and frequently referred to their feasts and traditions. Paul, who might be called the first interpreter of Jesus, was also Jewish, brought up as a Pharisee and completely dedicated to observance of the Torah, the Law of Moses. When he became a follower of Christ he did not cut himself off from his Jewish roots, rather he devoted himself to showing how Jesus was the fulfilment of all the hopes of the Jewish people. Other parts of the New Testament witness to styles of writing that are not easily comprehended today, for example apocalyptic and ancient biography. All this means that, while at first sight the New Testament might appear more accessible, there is much in it that requires explanation and interpretation. If our celebration of the Sunday Eucharist is to be meaningful and relevant then it is important for us to spend a little time trying to understand the readings. If we do this, either alone or in the company of others who are involved in preparing the liturgy, then we will come to a greater knowledge and love of Christ and our life of faith will be greatly enriched.

How did the New Testament come about?

Unlike the Old Testament period which covered centuries, the period for the life of Jesus of Nazareth and the emergence of the

Christian religion can be encompassed within 100 years. It is important to be aware that Christianity began as a sect within Judaism and that all the first Christians were Jews. Indeed the first crisis for the early Christian community concerned its approach to non-Jews who wanted to become members. St Paul who was preaching among Gentiles argued that they should be admitted simply through baptism. Others, however, wanted them to convert to Judaism first. This issue was resolved at the so-called council of Jerusalem and this move paved the way for Christianity to separate from Judaism and become a separate religion in its own right. The final separation between the two came about after the Jewish revolt against Roman rule that began in 66AD and ended in 70 with the destruction of the Jerusalem Temple. By that time Peter and Paul had both been martyred and the first gospel (Mark) had been written and was circulating among the Christian communities scattered between Jerusalem and Rome.

After the decision of the Council of Jerusalem in 49AD to allow Gentiles to be baptised, the Christian community continued to grow and its relations with Judaism were even more strained. The community in Jerusalem found itself more and more ostracised and even in need of help from the Gentile communities in Asia Minor and elsewhere. The Roman administration of Palestine went from bad to worse as a succession of governors failed to show any sympathy or sensitivity towards the Jews and their monotheistic religion. The situation finally came to a head in 66AD when the governor attempted to raid the temple treasury. This marked the beginning of a war that lasted four years. The Christians did not support this revolt and left Jerusalem. After some spectacular success against the Roman forces in Galilee in the early stages of the war, the emperor Nero sent his general Vespasian with a 60,000 strong army to crush the rebellion. He began in Galilee and by the year 68 things were turning against the Jews. Galilee was subdued and many who wished to continue the struggle fled to Jerusalem. With the death of Nero Vespasian became emperor and left his son Titus to finish the war. In 70 his Roman army laid siege to Jerusalem and after five months broke through the defences and destroyed the city including most of the temple.

With the end of their state and worship in the temple, the Jewish leaders now looked to the scriptures as the basis for worship and they also sought to rid Judaism of the 'sectarians', i.e. those Jews who called Jesus of Nazareth the Messiah. From this time on Jewish Christians were banned from the synagogue and Christians continued to develop their own worship and to gather their own scriptures (i.e. the letters of Paul and the gospels) while still making extensive use of the Greek translation of the Jewish Bible to show that Jesus was indeed the expected Messiah. By the end of Jewish War, the Christian church in Rome had already experienced a violent persecution under Nero who fixed the blame on them for the great fire of Rome. Many were arrested and publicly executed including Peter and Paul.

Before the end of the first century most of the writings of the New Testament were in circulation, though not bound together as one book. The process of gathering them into one collection took a little longer and when it was finished the content of the New Testament was as follows:

Four Gospels
One Acts of the Apostles
Thirteen Letters attributed to Paul
Eight general letters
One book of Revelation

All of these writings were in circulation among the Christian churches by the middle of the second century. However, it is known that there were other gospels and letters in circulation. How is it then that we have ended up with these? Who made the decision and when?

The first thing that must be said about the emergence of the Christian 'canon' (the list of approved books) is that it was not down to the decision of one individual at a particular time. The earliest known attempt to produce a New Testament was that of Marcion in 140AD. He believed that all of the Old Testament and much of the Christian material that was circulating was the product of a faith in a lesser creator god who was in fact evil. So to purge Christianity of this, he produced a Bible made up of a heavily edited gospel of Luke and ten of Paul's letters. His view was rejected by the early church and he was declared a heretic but in the period after this there was much debate and discussion about which books could be said to reflect the faith of the church founded by Jesus. During this debate there is a consistency about which books were in. The four gospels of Matthew, Mark, Luke and John were widely accepted as were the 13 letters of Paul. In certain places there was doubt about the others, including the book of Revelation, but by the end of the fourth century church councils in Carthage and Hippo showed that there was widespread agreement that the 27 books now in the New Testament should be accepted in the canon.

Raymond Brown, a noted Catholic scholar, suggests that for inclusion books had to meet the following three criteria:

1. Apostolic Origin. It was strongly felt that a given text should come from people who were or who lived in the company of the apostles.

2. Importance of the Christian communities who first received the writings. If it could be shown that the tradition of the writing went back to the first major centres of the spread of Christianity such as Antioch or Rome then books were deemed acceptable.

3. Conformity with the standard beliefs of the early Christian communities. So when a writing was being used to promote a teaching such as Jesus not being truly human it was not accepted.

The Content of the New Testament
The gospels of Matthew, Mark, Luke and John take pride of place in the collection though they were not the first Christian documents to be written. It is widely believed that Mark's was the first to be read and circulated. A comparison of Luke and Matthew indicates that these evangelists then made extensive use of Mark while also using other sources in writing their own gospels. Since all three make use of the same narrative framework they are called Synoptic (viewed from the same perspective). John, however, presents the story of Jesus in a very different manner. While he probably knew the traditions used by the other evangelists he chose to focus not on Jesus' preaching of the kingdom but instead on the person of Jesus himself and his identity as the Son of God, the Word made flesh. While the difference between John and the others is the most obvious, it is

very important to remember that each evangelist had his own theological insights and sought to address the needs of the Christian communities for whom he was writing. Mark wrote in the aftermath of Nero's persecution of the church in Rome, while Matthew is thought to have written mainly for Jewish Christians in Antioch in Syria. Luke, on the other hand, seems to address the needs of Gentile Christians perhaps somewhere in Greece. The vagueness about the background is due to the fact that none of the gospels gives information about who wrote it or where. What they all share is an enthusiasm to proclaim the good news of Jesus among the newly formed Christian communities. Each one witnesses to a vibrant faith that was transforming the lives of those who came in contact with it.

In addition to his gospel, Luke also wrote a companion volume, the Acts of the Apostles. It traces the development of the early church from its beginnings in Jerusalem to the last days of Paul in Rome. Luke goes to great lengths to show the continuity between the time of Jesus and the time of the church by showing how the same Holy Spirit empowers them both.

Paul and his Letters
Paul was born in Tarsus, a Roman city in the Province of Asia Minor (S.E. Turkey), possibly around the year 10AD. His Jewish name was Saul but as a Roman citizen he probably made use of its Latin form, Paul, especially when dealing with Gentiles (i.e. people of a non-Jewish background). His upbringing would have been typical of a Jew in the Diaspora, that is to say while he was reared in the practices and traditions of his faith he would also have received a typically Greek education, learning especially the art of rhetoric. In the Acts of the Apostles which gives us most of our information about Paul he is described as a tentmaker and it is clear that he made use of this trade during his missionary journeys. He says of himself that was very devout in the practice of his faith and we are told that as a young man he went to Jerusalem to study at the feet of Gamaliel, one of the greatest rabbis in the first century. His training was as a Pharisee. These were lay people who were devoted to a strict legal interpretation of the Law of Moses following their own oral traditions. In his public life Jesus had frequent arguments

with them over the correct interpretation of the scriptures and their legalistic attitude to the law. It is not known exactly when Paul came to Jerusalem as a young man but it may be imagined that it was soon after the death and resurrection of Jesus. At this point all the followers of Jesus were Jews and they began proclaiming to their fellow Jews that Jesus of Nazareth, who had been crucified as a criminal by the Romans, had risen from the dead and was indeed the long awaited Messiah of the Jewish people.

Paul's Conversion

The first preaching of the apostles caused division among the people and was perceived as dangerous by the authorities. One young Jew named Stephen, who like Paul was from outside Palestine, publicly proclaimed his faith in Jesus in a manner that led to his execution and it seems Paul was there in support of this repression (Acts 7:54-8:1). He even offered his services to the authorities who wanted to put down the message of Jesus, volunteering to go to Damascus to seek out his followers. It was on this journey that Paul had an experience of Jesus that was to radically alter not only his own life but also the whole development of the early church. The story of his conversion is told three times in the Acts (9:1-19, 22:4-16, 26:9-18) but Paul does not describe it in any of his own writings. In the letter he wrote to the Galatians Paul says that immediately after this experience he disappeared for three years to Arabia. Only after this time alone did he go to speak with Peter and the leaders of the church in Jerusalem.

Paul's mission to the Gentiles

From this time on he devoted himself to proclaiming the gospel, starting in the important city of Antioch in Syria. It was from here that he set out with two companions, Barnabas and John Mark to bring the message to Jewish communities in other cities (Acts 13-14). This journey led him to Cyprus and onwards to the Turkish mainland. While preaching in the local synagogues he received a mixed reception but among those who were very interested in his message were gentiles who were sympathetic to Jewish ideas on religion. Paul and his companions took it upon themselves to baptise these pagans and this action was to sow the seed for the first serious controversy in the early church.

The Council of Jerusalem

When some of the leaders in the church heard what was happening they wanted to put a stop to it, saying that before being baptised people should first become practising Jews. Paul strongly opposed this view and around 49AD attended a meeting in Jerusalem to debate the issue. Arguing from his experience of the Spirit at work among the gentiles, he showed that the message of Jesus was clearly for everyone and that the observance of the Jewish law should not be forced on his new converts. Paul's vigorous defence of his activity won the day and he was given approval to continue with his mission (Acts 15 and Gal 2:1-11).

This was a momentous decision for the early church as it meant that Christianity, which had been until now merely a sect within Judaism, would now begin to spread among non-Jews and become a new religion in its own right. Ironically this movement would be driven by a man who had persecuted the first Christians, hoping to stop the movement spreading even among the Jews. Paul was keenly aware of the paradox but also very aware of God's grace at work in him. In the years since he had come to a personal experience of God at work through the Spirit of Jesus, he grew in his understanding of the implications of this message for the whole world: 'There is no longer Jew or Greek, there is no longer slave or free, there is no longer male and female; for all of you are one in Christ Jesus.' (Gal 3:28) This insight would form the impetus for the rest of his mission and bring him to proclaim the gospel in Rome itself, the very heart of the pagan world.

Christianity in Europe

After the Council of Jerusalem Paul set off on what was to be his second missionary journey, this time joined by Silas and Timothy. It was the year 50AD and having visited some of the towns where he had preached earlier he felt called by God to cross over to Greece (Acts 16:9-10). Philippi was the first European town where they stopped to proclaim the gospel and there Paul met strong opposition from some pagans. He and Silas suffered a severe public beating at their hands and were then thrown into prison to await trial on charges of public disorder. Following a miraculous intervention in prison, and a confrontation with the authorities for arresting them illegally, they were asked to leave the town. Such a beginning was not promising but it is a measure of Paul's zeal that he would not be deterred from his calling to make known the message of Jesus. His next stop was to be Thessalonica and here too he ran into trouble, this time from some of the Jews of the town. However, even though his stay here was short it was enough to allow a community of believers to gather and it was to the Christians of Thessalonica that Paul would write his first letter, the earliest document in the New Testament.

Paul in Corinth
For his own safety he was urged to leave the region and so he headed south to Athens. His stay here was brief and in preaching terms appears to have been something of a failure. The intellectuals of Athens had little time for a message that proposed a doctrine of the resurrection of the dead (Acts 17:22-33) and so once again Paul was on the move, this time to the busy port city of Corinth. Here he was to have a very different experience. He met a Jewish Christian couple named Aquila and Priscilla and together with them preached the gospel not only in the synagogue but also among the Gentile inhabitants of the city. His stay here lasted some 18 months and by the time he left a thriving Christian community had developed there under his leadership. On leaving Corinth, Paul returned to Jerusalem for a short visit but was soon back on the road again.

His third missionary journey took Paul through places he had already worked but he also stopped in towns where Christian communities existed that he had not founded. This was the case with Ephesus and, as the Acts of the Apostles tells us, Paul spent time in this important city bringing the Christians there to a fuller understanding of what they had received (Acts 19). His influence was such that local silversmiths who made their living out of creating images of the goddess Artemis, the pagan deity of the city, began to protest that Paul was destroying their livelihood. This led to a near riot and as a result Paul moved on but not before he had encouraged the local leaders to continue with their mission. The last part of his journey was spent in the regions around the Aegean Sea, visiting such places as Troas and Miletus before going back to Jerusalem. It was during this third journey (53-56AD) that he wrote some of his most important letters including those to the churches in Rome and Corinth. His epistle to the Christians in Rome was to let of them know that he intended visiting them. However, at the time of writing he did not realise he would indeed be coming to them but not as he had expected.

Paul's last journey
On his return to Jerusalem Paul found himself once again embroiled in controversy. Some Jews accused him of undermining their religion and the temple and a mob set about beating him. He was only saved from death by the intervention of the Roman authorities. However, the leaders of the Jews demanded that he should face trial and at this point Paul invoked the fact that he was a Roman citizen and therefore was entitled to a trial in Rome. He was left a prisoner in Caesarea, some 100 kms north west of Jerusalem, for over two years before he was sent under guard to be tried in Rome. His eventful journey is described in Acts 27-28 and, having finally arrived, Paul was held under house arrest. Some of his other important letters were probably written at this time including the letters to the Philippians and Colossians. No details are given in the New Testament as to how he died. The Acts of the Apostles ends with him encouraging the faithful in Rome and teaching, but it is believed that he was martyred during the persecution of the church initiated by Nero sometime around 62/63AD.

Although 13 letters are attributed to Paul in the New Testament, not all of them are thought to have been penned by the apostle. There is general agreement about 1&2 Corinthians, Galatians, Romans, 1 Thessalonians, Philippians and Philemon while there is some dispute about the others. Scholars suggest that they may have been written by his disciples or under his direction. We know that Paul made use of secretaries (cf Romans 16:22) and on occasions made a point of writing a conclusion in his own hand (2 Thess 3:17, Gal 6:11, 1 Cor 16:21). 1&2 Titus and Timothy portray a church at a later period in its development, while Colossians and Ephesians indicate a doctrine which seems to go beyond his thought as expressed in the 'genuine' letters. Notwithstanding these discussions, all the letters are considered as inspired scripture and take their place equally in the canon of the New Testament. In his writing, Paul rarely makes reference to incidents from the life of Jesus. He is more concerned to draw out the implications of faith in Jesus for the communities and the particular situations in which they find themselves. His influence in the early church was enormous as is evidenced by the reference to his letters in the second letter of Peter which seems to speak of them as scripture (2 Peter 3:15-16). The letters tend to follow a particular format, though each of them has its own character because of the specific problems Paul is dealing with. The format is pretty much as follows:

Introduction/Greeting
Thanksgiving
Body of letter
Exhortation
Conclusion.

Other New Testament Writings
The other letters in the New Testament display similar characteristics but are sometimes called the 'Catholic' epistles. They are ascribed to Peter, James and John but here again there are disagreements about exactly who wrote them. It is clear that there is a connection between the gospel and letters of John. They appear to have a similar audience in mind and to share similar views about the identity of Jesus and what it means to be a disciple. The so-called Letter to the Hebrews is listed with the others but in form and content it bears no resemblance to a letter. It is rather an elaborate sermon, carefully prepared by an unknown author with a view to explaining to Jewish Christians the consequences for their faith of accepting Jesus as the fulfilment of their hopes.

The last book of the New Testament is the Book of Revelation. Because it is much used by fundamentalists and groups predicting the end of the world, this wonderful work is frequently avoided by many Christians. There can be no doubt that it is difficult to understand but once its genre is recognised, and this determines the interpretation, it can be appreciated as a ingenious symbolic meditation on Christ's victory over sin and evil. It is steeped in Old Testament symbolism and it exudes a wonderful hope and joy rooted in an awareness of the abiding presence of the risen Christ with the church.

The Season of Advent

THE FIRST SUNDAY OF ADVENT

First Reading: Isaiah 63:16-17, 64:1, 3-8

Purple is the liturgical colour for the season of Advent and that is a reminder to us that it is a time of repentance. Our preparation for the birth of the Saviour must involve recognition of our need of him and of the ways in which we have turned away from him. This reading from Isaiah is very well suited to that purpose for it is a direct appeal to God that he should visit his people once again and save them from their sins. The basis for the appeal is that as the chosen people, God has created them; they are his children, he is their Father. In the past he has come to save them, so could he not now 'tear open the heavens and come down?' There is a contrite acceptance of their misdeeds but also a plea for compassion: 'We are the clay and you are the potter, we are all the work of your hand.' These words from Isaiah come from the last section of this long book and relate to a time when, after their return from exile, there was a sense of disappointment among the people that things had not improved dramatically. The prophet gives voice to their longing for God and in so doing makes the connection between the need to change our outlook if we really do wish to welcome the Lord.

Second Reading: 1 Corinthians 1:3-9

As we ended the liturgical year thinking about the second coming of Christ, so we begin the new year on the same theme. Advent is initially a looking forward Christ's return before it becomes a looking back to his birth. So in this reading from Paul he writes to the young church in Corinth thanking God that they have been blessed in so many ways. This means that they will be able to live the Christian life they are called to as they await the last day. As always, Paul is keenly aware that this new life in Christ is only possible because we have been joined to him through baptism. The context for his words is the belief that the second coming of Christ will be soon and even though this was a mistaken view, the appeal to be true to our baptism is as valid as ever. This work has been begun by God our Father and 'he is faithful' so there is no cause for anxiety or concern as we try to live out our daily lives in the power of the Spirit.

Gospel: Mark 13:33-37
It is widely thought that Mark's was the first gospel to be written and that it was composed in Rome just after Nero's extremely violent persecution of the Christians of that city. One of the themes in Mark is that Jesus is a crucified Messiah and that being faithful to him will involve suffering for your beliefs. This means that they must always be vigilant and that is the theme of today's gospel. It is taken from chapter 13 which is a link between the end of Jesus' public ministry and the beginning of the passion and it stresses the importance of believers not becoming lethargic or casual. The fact is we live in a changing world and new demands will be made on us as followers of Christ. For Mark's first readers that meant being persecuted by the most powerful government in the world. For us, at this time of year, the threat to our faith may be from a more subtle yet no less destructive enemy of the gospel – rampant consumerism.

Reflection
When the prophet prayed that God might 'tear open the heavens and come down' he was probably thinking in terms of what had happened on Mt Sinai many years before when the Israelites experienced God in the awesome splendour of nature (Ex19). It would have been unimaginable for the prophet that God should indeed immerse himself totally in our world and yet in the fullness of time that is precisely what did happen. While Isaiah prayed that the mountains would melt like wax at the presence of God, it seems God was more interested in melting our hearts. It is as though the Potter became the clay. During Advent we are invited to think about our human weakness, not so as to become sad or depressed but so that we can be filled with wonder at the way in which God chooses to save us.

THE SECOND SUNDAY OF ADVENT

First Reading: Isaiah 40:1-5, 9-11
Chapter 40 of the Book of the Prophet Isaiah marks the beginning of prophecies which come from a later time than the first
section. For this reason this part of the book is sometimes known
as Second Isaiah. These writings refer to the time when the
Israelites who have been exiled in Babylon receive word that
they are to be allowed to return home. They are full of hope and
gratitude and portray the God of Israel as the Lord of creation
and the Lord of history who has not abandoned his people but
who will lead them across the wilderness to Jerusalem. The
theme of today's reading is consolation. The people who have
known the pain of war and separation from their homeland hear
words of comfort as God announces a new day for them. The
desert wasteland which stretches for hundreds of miles between
Babylon and Jerusalem will be transformed into a highway revealing the glory of their God who is both a warrior who fights
on behalf of his people and a shepherd who nourishes them and
guides them to rest.

Second Reading: 2 Peter 3:8-14
One of the most important themes of Advent is that of looking
forward to the second coming of Jesus and that is the theme addressed in this reading. Although the letter is attributed to Peter,
many scholars believe that it comes from a time after the martyrdom of the apostle when some Christian communities were
troubled by the delay in the *parousia* or second coming. In the
verses we hear today the writer explains the delay in the Lord's
coming as evidence of his patience, for he wants everybody to
come to repentance so that nobody will be lost. However, the
end, when it does come, will be unexpected and the only way to
be prepared is to live in a way which is worthy of our Christian
calling. The end of the world as we know it will be the beginning
of 'the new heavens and the new earth', a time when we will live
in harmony with one another and with God.

Gospel: Mark 1:1-8
The consoling words of the first reading are read again in the

gospel. Only this time the way being prepared is not the return journey from exile in Babylon but the path to our hearts as John the Baptist calls the people to repentance in preparation for the arrival of Jesus. Like one of the Old Testament prophets, John is radical in his commitment to his calling and the description of him as wearing camel skin clothing and eating locusts and wild honey echoes the portrayal of Elijah in 2 Kings 1:8. In the first century there were a variety of views as to how God would act on behalf of his people. Many hoped for dramatic intervention and stunning military victories, but John's focus was on their need to repent, in other words to change their worldview and to live accordingly. In this way they would leave themselves open to what God would do through Jesus who, though more powerful than John, would come among them as a servant.

Reflection
The call to repentance lies at the heart of the Advent season. Like the people of John's time we too long for a better world and a time when suffering will cease. However, such a change will not come by the waving of a divine magic wand. It will come when we prepare ourselves for it, when we open our minds and hearts to the gift that is offered to us at Christmas. It is not a call for sentimentality about the child in the manger, it a radical call to change and that is never easy. That is why Advent is such an appropriate time to celebrate the sacrament of reconciliation. There we encounter the all-embracing love of God who never ceases to offer us new life and hope and who empowers us to be his instruments for change in a world torn apart by selfishness and greed. What better way could there be to prepare the way of the Lord in the wilderness of our hearts?

THE THIRD SUNDAY OF ADVENT

First Reading: Isaiah 61:1-2, 10-11
In order to appreciate the importance of the first verses of this reading we only have to realise that they are the ones chosen by Jesus to explain his calling to the people in the synagogue in Nazareth (Lk 4:16-18). The prophet uses the theme of the Year of the Lord's favour, that is the Jubilee Year, to show what God in-

tends for the people. The Jubilee was an event occurring every fifty years which gave the people an opportunity to make a fresh start (see Lev 25:8-55). Debts were cancelled, slaves were freed and those driven off the land by poverty had a chance to return home. The prophet points to God's presence with the people by telling them that he has been anointed to proclaim this year of grace. The response to such good news is likened to the joy experienced by a bride and groom on their wedding day for the prophet recognises in this action the renewal of God's covenant love, a time when everyone can rediscover their true dignity as children of God.

Second Reading: 1 Thessalonians 5:16-24
In this reading from the end of the letter we return to the Advent theme of waiting. Once again Paul is speaking of the second coming of Christ but the advice he gives to the young church at Thessalonica fits well with our season. Waiting for Jesus is not some passive exercise, it is rather an active pursuit of the things that God asks of us. Therefore we are urged to pray constantly and to be happy but we must understand that these exhortations are not something that we can respond to by our own willpower. As we might expect from Paul, the importance of the role of the Holy Spirit is stressed; there can be no authentic Christian living without the gift of the Spirit. It is the Spirit which allows us to discern what is right and good and which enables us to carry out our good intentions. An awareness of the Spirit within allows us to pray and to be truly content.

Gospel: John 1:6-8, 19-28
From now until after Christmas we leave Mark's gospel, but nonetheless for today the focus remains on John the Baptist. As in Mark, John's gospel has no story of the birth of Jesus but right from the outset it emphasises the divine origin of Jesus, the light of the world, the Word made flesh. The role of the Baptist is to bear witness to who Jesus really is and that is what we see in the text for today. John always directs the focus away from himself and points to the one who is coming, and once again the quotation from Is 40 is heard. The level of expectation is high, as can be seen from the questions being put to John but his only interest

is pointing the way to Jesus and that makes him a perfect role model for Advent.

Reflection

In the gospel John the Baptist describes Jesus as 'standing among you, unknown to you'. In John's time this was because Jesus had not yet begun his ministry, but in our own day these words have a particular relevance. We live by faith in Jesus the crucified and risen Lord present in our world. In preparing for Christmas we want to renew our awareness of that presence and to help others be aware of it. In Advent we, like John, are called to be witnesses to the light he brings. In small but important ways we can bring light into the lives of those around us. Simple acts of kindness, sharing our time, talents or resources with those in need, is the only way Christ's light will shine for many people this Christmas. In our time, through the gift of the Spirit, the Word becomes flesh in us.

THE FOURTH SUNDAY OF ADVENT

First Reading: 2 Samuel 7;1-5, 8-12, 16

The Books of Samuel in the Old Testament tell the story of the transition from the times of the Judges in Israel to the beginnings of the monarchy. That the people should have wanted a king was seen as a lack of faith on their part for the Lord Yahweh was king in Israel. Saul, who was the first king, fared badly but things improved with David and in the section we read from today David has united the people and defeated their enemies. He then turns his attention to the fact that while he, as king, lives in a palace, the Ark of the Covenant still dwells in a tent and he resolves to build a temple. However, God has different ideas and the prophet Nathan is sent to David with a message reminding the king that it is not his place to make such a decision. God has journeyed with his people through all the ups and downs of their history and has no need of a temple. In fact, now, at this time it is God who will build David a 'house', for he promises that the descendants of David will rule in Israel. This prophecy would take on great significance centuries later when the Jews had no king and no one from the line of David ruled. The people began to look forward to a messiah, i.e. God's anointed who would be of the house of David and who would deliver Israel from her enemies. This is why in the New Testament much time is given to showing that Jesus is of the house of David.

Second Reading: Romans 16:25-27
With this reading we are at the conclusion of the letter and it ends as it began with the praise of God. Paul has explained his thinking about Jesus and why he has devoted his life to proclaiming the good news to the pagans or Gentiles. Now as he draws this long letter to a close, he gives praise to God for Jesus who reveals the plan of God which has been hidden for so long. Now this plan is clear to all and it includes the salvation of everyone. This insight is a cause of great joy to Paul and is the driving force in his ministry. It shows the wisdom of God which is beyond any human philosophy and is the reason why we should all be caught up in the praise of the Almighty.

Gospel: Luke 1:26-38
If John the Baptist dominates the early part of Advent, it is Mary the mother of Jesus who comes centre stage now. In this text from Luke, our attention is focused on the event upon which the mystery of God's saving will depends. Throughout the scriptures, God has sought out people with humility and courage to hear and respond to his word and through them his saving will has been made known. In this young woman from Nazareth the human response to God finds its perfect model. Luke presents Mary as the woman of faith and he gives more prominence to her than the other evangelists. By her openness to the Spirit of God she opens the way for God to come into the world and that is the way Luke presents discipleship. God will be at work in the world wherever the followers of Jesus leave themselves open to the work of his Spirit in an attitude of faith.

Reflection
It's a little ironic that David should have imagined that he could do something for God. It seems that his success as king went to his head and he forgot his humble origins as a shepherd boy. In

the gospel for today we see an Israelite who is fully aware of who she is before her God and it is this humility which allows her to say 'yes'. The promise made to David in the grandeur of his palace centuries before would now be fulfilled because an ordinary girl in ordinary surroundings has an extraordinary openness to her God. There is very little splendour and majesty in the Christmas story; it is characterised by simplicity and humility and these are the gifts we need to appreciate the power of its message. Let's pray for them with faith and fervour.

The Feast of Christmas

The Readings for the Masses of Christmas are the same for each year of the liturgical cycle

THE VIGIL MASS

First Reading: Is 62:1-5
The original setting for this reading was the return of the Jewish exiles from Babylon. The whole experience of war and deportation had been a painful reminder to the people of their failure to live according to the ways of the covenant but now God speaks to them again about the desire of his heart which is that they should come to know their true worth and how much their God longs to be one with them, just like a bridegroom longs for his bride. The sending of God's son is the ultimate proof that God wants us to know our true worth.

Second Reading: Acts 13:16-17, 22-25
In this reading we read a section of a speech given by Paul during his first missionary journey. The town of Antioch in Pisidia was situated in what is now S.W. Turkey and, as was customary for Paul when he came to a town, he preached first in the synagogue to the local Jewish population. Appropriately for today he preaches that Jesus is indeed the fulfilment of the long awaited promise made by God that a son of David would be their Messiah and Saviour.

Gospel: Matthew 1:1-25
It is suggested that the short form of this gospel may be used, namely verses 18-25. The reason is clear enough as these tell Matthew's account of how Jesus was born to Mary and Joseph in Bethlehem. Matthew emphasises that Jesus is the fulfilment of the scriptures, especially the important verse in Isaiah 7:14. He explains that the child will be called Jesus (Hebrew *Joshua*) because this name means God saves, but in the quotation we are given another name 'Emmanuel' – God is with us. The two are fitting for Jesus because one describes what he does and the other who he is. The earlier part of the reading, giving the genealogy of Jesus, is Matthew's way of affirming that the God

who guided the people of Israel through all their troubled history is active in the birth of Jesus. Just as some of Jesus' ancestors were born in unusual or even scandalous circumstances, so too Jesus comes in an unexpected way.

MIDNIGHT MASS

First Reading: Isaiah 9:1-7
The historical setting for this passage is towards the end of the reign of king Ahaz of Judah. The people have been through years of warfare and bloodshed and the threat of invasion by Assyria remains. Into this situation comes the king's son Hezekiah and the prophet Isaiah sees in him a brighter future in which the oppression of recent years ceases and the people can look forward to a time of peace and justice. While the reign of king Hezekiah was an improvement on what went before, it still proved to be a disappointment and so in later years the prophet's words came to be seen as a reference to an ideal king. The early church saw in this text a prophecy about Jesus, the son of David who revealed himself as Mighty God and Prince of Peace. The people who have walked in darkness are all those who have waited for God's intervention in the history of the world and now they can rejoice because on this holy night a 'child is born for us'. The imagery is rooted in the change that is brought about when war ends and a new day dawns and so it captures perfectly the longing that still exists for a time when all people can live in peace and that is surely the heart of our prayer at Christmas.

Second reading: The Letter of Paul to Titus 2:11-14
Titus, who was charged with the care of the church in Crete, had been a fellow worker with Paul and in this letter he is encouraged to be faithful to his task and to preserve the community from the false teaching which would distort the message of the gospel. These verses are appropriate for today because they remind us that even at Christmas it is the work of Christ as risen Saviour that we recall and the stress is on our response to him. Welcoming the child born in a stable means more than mere sentiment. Our lives must change as we continue to hope for his return among us.

Gospel: Luke 2:1-14

Luke puts his account of the birth of Jesus in the context of the rule of the emperor Augustus. He is the ruler of the world and the one credited with bringing peace to the empire, yet now in the humblest of circumstances a child is born whose rule will never end and whose power derives not from military might nor economic wealth. He is the true Saviour whose birth is a cause of joy in heaven and on earth and is first announced to the disenfranchised.

THE DAWN MASS

First Reading: Isaiah 62:11-12

This short reading, taken from the near the end of the Book of the Prophet Isaiah, returns to a favourite theme of the prophet: the faithfulness of God who more than anything wants to save his people from all that would keep them from knowing that they are indeed his beloved children. The daughter of Zion is a reference to the people of Jerusalem, the city of God that for too long has suffered the consequences of war and violence. New names are given here to symbolise the true identity of God's chosen people.

Second Reading: Titus 3:4-7

Again in this reading the Christmas message is presented to us in terms of the whole story of the good news. God's gift of his Son and the pouring out of his Holy Spirit are based solely on the compassion of the Father. The birth of Jesus is the setting in motion of this one great act of God by which we might come to know our true worth. This is why Christmas is such a wonderful feast.

Gospel: Luke 2:15-20

This is a continuation of the gospel used at midnight Mass and tells how the shepherds went immediately to Bethlehem. There they find things as the angels had told them. The gospel offers two responses to the unfolding story. One is that of Mary who 'treasured all these things and pondered them in her heart' and the other is that of the shepherds who went away glorifying and praising God. As people of faith participating in this feast we are invited to do the same. Christmas is a time for praise and thanksgiving to God but it is also an invitation to reflect deeply on the mystery that is being put before us.

MASS DURING THE DAY

First Reading: Isaiah 52:7-10
Once again the writings of Isaiah are called upon to bring out the meaning of Christmas and this time we are presented with a message of salvation aimed at the war-weary citizens of Jerusalem. After the failure of so many human kings to guide them in the way of peace, now, at last, God himself their warrior king is coming to console his people and to rule over them.

Second Reading: Hebrews 1:1-6
The opening verses of the Letter to the Hebrews sum up in a very simple yet profound way how the early church viewed the coming of Christ. While the prophets of old spoke in a powerful way about the saving will of God and his faithfulness, they never imagined how that will would be finally accomplished and that faithfulness displayed. This is the amazing truth that has been revealed in the person of Jesus who is 'the radiant light of God's glory' and who is therefore greater than any angel or prophet.

Gospel: John 1:1-18
The gospel of John has no account of the birth of Jesus; rather the evangelist chooses to begin his story with a poem and that is the gospel for this Mass. Rather than considering the life of Jesus from the time of his birth, John seeks to find and explore his identity by meditating on Jesus as the Word made Flesh. The Jews to whom the good news was first preached were very familiar with the idea of the word of God through their oral and written traditions. For generations God had made himself and his saving will known to them through his word and now that word becomes human, and as a human being reveals the glory of God in a way that is beyond our wildest imaginings. This is a staggering claim and one that many then and indeed still today

find too hard to believe. Yet it is the very heart of the Christmas message. Throughout the gospel of John the Word made Flesh reveals God through the signs he does and each of them shows that God's greatest desire is that we should have life and have it in its fullness.

Reflection

There is a remarkable variety in the twelve readings that are given for the Christmas Masses. One of the most striking things about them is that only three of them actually tell the Christmas story. The other nine are taken from both Old and New Testaments and in different ways invite reflection on the feast that is being celebrated. They all challenge us to move beyond the sentiment of the nativity play and to make our own this remarkable truth that we dare not believe. By the 'flesh taking' of God's eternal Word everybody and everything is made sacred and if we accept this then we must live differently in the world for it really is a beautiful and a holy place and all the cruelty and injustice that surround us cannot be allowed to erase that.

THE FEAST OF THE HOLY FAMILY

First Reading: Genesis 15:1-6, 21:1-3

This reading is made up of two parts, showing God's promise to Sarah and Abraham regarding a son and its fulfilment with the birth of Isaac. The reading is relevant for the season of Christmas because it emphasises that God is true to his word and the importance of having faith. God's promise to Abraham formed the basis of the first covenant and the apparent delay in fulfilling the promise seemed to raise doubts about whether God could succeed in granting the old man a son. Indeed that is the theme of the first part of today's reading. Abraham (still called Abram in this section) seems to question God. The scene takes place at night and this is no doubt symbolic of Abraham's difficulty in seeing the way ahead since he has no son. God invites him to ponder the night sky and to see in the myriad stars a sign of his many descendants. Once again Abraham puts his trust in God and, as we discover in the second part of the reading, after many difficulties and trials his wife Sarah does conceive and bear a son.

Second Reading: Hebrews 11:8, 11-12, 17-19
The letter to the Hebrews is one of the most difficult writings of the New Testament for the modern reader. Although tradition-ally attributed to Paul, very few today would hold that it comes from him. In fact little is known about when, where or to whom it was written yet it contains some of the most profound insights into the meaning of the death of Jesus to be found in the New Testament. The section for today connects very well with the first reading as it celebrates Abraham and Sarah as our ancestors in faith. At this point the author is encouraging his Jewish-Christian readers to follow their example and to renew their faith in Jesus as the long awaited messiah, the son of the promise.

We may deduce from the letter that because of the difficulties they were experiencing they were tempted to abandon the Christian community and to return to the certainty of the old days. The author reminds them that faith is not about having all the answers or indeed certain knowledge; it is much more about putting one's whole life into God's hands. This is precisely what all the great heroes of the Bible had to do

Gospel: Luke 2:22-40
Since the gospel of Mark has no infancy narrative or reference to the early life of Jesus, the gospel for today's feast is taken from Luke and it reports the wonderfully moving scene of Mary and Joseph bringing their newborn son to the temple to consecrate him to the Lord. In the plan of Luke's gospel it is important be-cause it stresses the value of the faithful piety of those Jews who waited with abiding trust in God for the coming of the re-deemer. Simeon and Anna are put before us as models of patient endurance whose whole lives have been directed towards God and who have trusted in his saving will. This attitude has al-ready been evident in the response of Mary and Joseph to all that has taken place and it will continue to characterise their lives as they return to Nazareth and watch their son grow to maturity in a world that will reject him.

Reflection
In the gospel for today we see Mary and Joseph presenting their newborn son to God in the temple. It was a symbolic gesture

pointing to the reality of their faith. Just like all those who had gone before them in faith, this young couple were being asked to put their trust in God. It was not easy then and now in the twenty-first century with all our reliance on knowledge, certainty and contracts, it is still not easy. Going into the third millennium the Christian family needs to stand out as a sign to the world that to be truly human we must not try to play God but rather be willing put our trust in the God revealed in the holy family of Nazareth.

THE SECOND SUNDAY AFTER CHRISTMAS

First Reading: Ecclesiasticus 24:1-2, 8-12
The Book of Ecclesiasticus, also known by its Hebrew name Sirach, is one of the last books of wisdom writing in the Old Testament dating from around 200BC. By this stage the other books of the Bible were already widely revered and used in the liturgy of the temple and synagogues. The author of this book wished to reflect on the great traditions of his people especially as exemplified in the Torah, or Law. He does this from the perspective of the wisdom books which saw wisdom as not just the fruit of experience but primarily as a gift of God. In the text we read today he identifies the gift of wisdom which was with God from the beginning, with the gift of the Torah which was given to Moses on Mount Sinai. The text is important for the Christmas season because of God's command to wisdom: 'Pitch your tent in Jacob.' The same expression is used to describe the incarnation in the fourth gospel: 'The Word became flesh and pitched his tent among us.' So the writers of the New Testament took the Old Testament tradition about wisdom to explain that Jesus was indeed the embodiment of God's wisdom.

Second Reading: Ephesians 1:3-6, 15-18
The letter to the Ephesians differs from some of Paul's other writings in that its theme addresses questions that are relevant to the whole church and not just issues faced by a particular community as is the case with 1 Corinthians or Galatians. The opening chapter from which we read today is a wonderful prayer of thanks and praise to God for all that he has done for us

through Christ. Paul recognises that in Christ every possible spiritual blessing has been poured out on those who believe. Through him we have become the children of God in a very unique way. Paul sees this borne out in the behaviour of the community who show great love towards each other and so his prayer for them is that they will have the wisdom to understand what it is God has done for them. He prays that this wisdom will in turn bring them to a full knowledge of God and the great hope that their Christian calling holds for them.

Gospel: John 1:1-18
This is the text used for the Christmas day Mass *(see above)*.

Reflection
With these readings we are reminded again just how profoundly beautiful the Season of Christmas is. All human life is given a dignity which, if we take time to reflect upon it, transforms our understanding of ourselves and the world in which we live. The light breaks through into our fragile human hearts and shows us what is possible if we only have the courage to believe in what God has done and continues to do for us through his Son, the Word made Flesh. The evangelist who penned the gospel for today did not come to the insight he shares with us on his first encounter with Jesus, nor even immediately after the resurrection. Rather these words are the fruit of many years of prayer and reflection on the mystery of the person of Christ. As such they are a reminder to us that we too must engage with this mystery through prayer and reflection if we really want to make our own the gift that God gives us in the person of his Son. Paul, who was steeped in the Jewish tradition which attached great importance to the study of the scriptures, knew how central it was for his converts to Christ to understand the religion which they had embraced. So in this new year, if you are still wondering about what resolution to make, it might be a good idea to take steps to grow in your understanding of your faith. Many Christian adults do no study of, or reflection on their faith after they leave school and this means that their religion can easily become a matter of habit or ritual. Decide today to do something about it – and persuade a friend to come with you!

The Season of Lent

THE FIRST SUNDAY OF LENT

First Reading: Genesis 9:8-15
Our journey through the Season of Lent begins very early in the story of God's desire to bring humanity back from the path of sin. The Book of Genesis opens with the wonder of an entirely good creation in harmony with God and itself. This situation changes because human beings choose to ignore their limit-ations but despite this God does not give up. In today's reading God speaks to Noah after the flood and in words which echo the blessing to Adam and Eve in chapter 1 God commits himself again to a life-giving relationship with Noah and his descend-ants, in other words, with the whole human race. The rainbow becomes the symbol of a covenant whereby God pledges never again to flood the earth and destroy the world. This is the first covenant in the Bible and opens the way to the history of salv-ation in which the plan of God is gradually revealed to the chosen people and which will culminate in the gift of his own Son who will inaugurate the new and everlasting covenant.

Second Reading: 1 Peter 3:18-28
These verses from the First Letter of Peter take up the imagery of the first reading in order to explain to newly baptised Christians the profound significance of the sacrament they have received. Peter highlights the importance of the symbolism of water by pointing to the story of Noah and the ark. Even though water was the cause of death to the sinners, it was also the means by which Noah and his family were saved and began a new life. In the water of baptism we put to death all that is not of God and rise out of the water to a new life in Christ. The 'Dominations and Powers' spoken about at the end of the reading refer to a way of understanding the world in which between the human and divine realms there exist forces which work in ways op-posed to the plan of God. In the New Testament the authors saw these forces as being totally overpowered as a result of the resur-rection of Jesus.

Gospel: Mark 1:12-15

The gospel for the First Sunday of Lent is always the story of the temptation in the wilderness, and in Mark the account is particularly brief. That said, it is remarkable what the evangelist can pack into just three verses. In the scene just prior to this, Jesus has heard the voice of God telling him that he is the beloved son and in the strength of this affirmation we now see Jesus 'driven' out into the wilderness. One of the characteristics of Mark is a sense of urgency throughout the narrative. Things move quickly as the mystery of the kingdom present in the person of Jesus unfolds. We are told that in the wilderness for forty days Jesus was tempted but we are not told how. However, the language echoes the Old Testament story of the chosen people and their desert experience of testing. Jesus in his life, death and resurrection confronts and is victorious over the power of evil. After his testing he returns and begins his ministry with one simple appeal: 'Repent and believe the good news.' This appeal sets the tone for our observance of Lent as we make ourselves available to God through our mini desert experience.

Reflection

The challenge that is put to us not just this week but every time we gather is to believe the good news. We are not being told to perform heroic deeds of self-sacrifice or to overcome and master our sinfulness; no, we are being challenged to really hear and believe that through baptism we have become children of God and that God says to each of us: 'You are my beloved.' It is hard to really accept this and there are many voices that try to convince us that it is not the truth. So Lent is a wonderful opportunity to rediscover our worth and the wonder of coming to life in Christ. The readings today challenge us not to focus on storm clouds but to see in the rainbow the beautiful faithfulness of God. Let that be the focus of all we undertake during this season of repentance.

THE SECOND SUNDAY OF LENT

First Reading: Genesis 22:1-2, 9-13, 15-18
At the outset of the Abraham story in Genesis 12, God told him to go to the land that he would show him and thus began Abraham's great journey of faith. He was promised that he would become the father of a great nation and, after many threats to the promise and years of disappointment, Isaac his son was finally born to Sarah in her old age. So now when the promise of God at last appears to have been fulfilled, God speaks once again and tells Abraham to go to another place, only this time he is to bring his beloved son with and offer him as a sacrifice. Once again Abraham sets out to do as God asks of him, no doubt completely bewildered and utterly heart-broken. Only at the last minute does he discover that God does not want the sacrifice of his son but rather he wanted to know whether indeed Abraham was capable of the complete surrender of faith. Could he in all circumstances call out to God: 'Here I am Lord'? Abraham was not found wanting and so pointed the way for all who would walk the path of faith.

Second Reading: Romans 8:31-34
Paul, as a devout Jew, was well aware of the story of the sacrifice of Isaac and knew that God did not want the death of Abraham's beloved son. He also knew that God did not want the death of his own beloved Son either, but since the cross was the consequence of being faithful to his mission, God the Father accepted the sacrifice of Jesus. In this, Paul saw the ultimate proof of God's love for sinful humanity and pleads with his readers to understand just what this means. If God was willing to give up his Son will he then deny us anything? Jesus' death on the cross issued in the new life of the resurrection and it is the risen Lord who intercedes for us in heaven.

Gospel: Mark 9:2-10
The gospel for the Second Sunday of Lent each year is the account of the transfiguration of Jesus. In Mark we have just passed the half way point and Jesus has revealed to the disciples that he is the Messiah but he wishes them to come to understand

this not in terms of glory and esteem but in being faithful to God's will and so he has mentioned to them for the first time that he will have to endure his passion in Jerusalem. Peter is appalled at the idea but Jesus does not shrink from telling him that those who want to follow must take up their cross. This is the background to today's gospel. Peter, James and John who were present at the raising of the daughter of Jairus (chapter 6) are now invited up the mountain where they behold him quite literally in a whole new light. At this key moment of revelation of who he really is they are invited to 'listen to him'. However, as the story continues we learn that they are poor listeners and they fail to take on board his message of the self-emptying love of the kingdom. The next time these three are invited to come aside with him is at the foot of a mountain, the Mount of Olives, in the Garden of Gethsemane, and there too Jesus is revealed to them, not in glory but in suffering and, because they have not listened, they will run away.

Reflection

Lent is a time for letting go and these readings make the point very well. If we are to come to know God and the meaning of real love, then we must learn to let go of our certainties and insisting on having things our own way. Abraham and Jesus both learned to entrust everything into the hands of God the Father, even when this appeared to lead to the end of everything they had hoped for. God in Jesus would have us understand that he is with us in every moment of our lives and each moment, whether at the top of the mountain or in Gethsemane, is sacred. If we are to understand this, we must develop the art of doing what the Father has asked us and that is the art of listening, really listening to his Son.

THE THIRD SUNDAY OF LENT

First Reading: Exodus 20:1-17

The Ten Commandments are probably the best known words from the Old Testament and in this reading we find the full version from the book of Exodus which outlines the reasoning behind the commandment to rest on the Sabbath and the prohibition of images. While many people are familiar with these laws given by God to Moses on Mt Sinai, they are not usually thought of in relation to their context which is the saving event by which Israel was liberated from slavery. In giving the commandments God is offering to the chosen people a charter by which they can live in true freedom. These are not the guidelines for a personal morality but rather offer the way for a new society to grow based on respect for the dignity and rights of others. They are given in the context of a covenant relationship, one that binds God to the Israelites and the Israelites to their God. As such the covenant is the next step in the history of salvation, for by adhering to the demands of this law the chosen people can come to an awareness of the kind of world their God wants. Jesus, in preaching the kingdom, will take this law even further developing it into the commandment of universal love.

Second Reading: 1 Corinthians 1:22-25
In these verses Paul is contrasting the two ways in which the Jew and the Gentile would expect to find God. The Jews look to their history and point to the great miracles of the past to show the presence of God with them. Those influenced by Greek culture on the other hand, point to the value of philosophical reasoning in the effort to come to knowledge of God. Paul, however, points out that the preaching of the gospel makes no sense to either party because it proclaims a crucified messiah. This was an utterly scandalous idea to the Jews and just pure foolishness from a philosophical point of view. Yet it is precisely in the weakness of the cross that the greatness of God's love can be seen. Instead of showing his presence by a glorious miracle, God had chosen to identify with the poor and the suffering. It is in the events of Good Friday that the true power and wisdom of God can be seen.

Gospel: John 2:13-25
For the next three Sundays the gospel will be taken from John and will set before us the way in which the fourth evangelist understands the mystery of the cross and resurrection. Of all the evangelists, John relies most heavily on symbolism to communicate the meaning of Easter and what it reveals to us about God

and the story for today is no exception. On the face of it what Jesus did in cleansing the temple was a rejection of corrupt practices in the temple that distracted from true worship of God. But there is more at stake in his dramatic gesture and this becomes apparent as Jesus responds to the authorities who oppose him. The real issue here is the true worship of God and that will come about through the death and resurrection of Jesus, for as the Word made flesh he is the true temple or dwelling place of God and in him we will come to abide in God's love, which is what true worship is all about.

Reflection

With the passage of time and the familiarity of the cross or crucifix as a religious symbol it may be that we have lost the sense of what Paul and John are saying. We almost seem comfortable with the idea of a crucified Lord. Perhaps the scandal it contains would be clearer to us if we used the used the symbol of a gallows or an electric chair. Ever since Good Friday our faith is not in God the miracle-worker but in the God who chose to be known through weakness and vulnerability. The love of the new and everlasting covenant is to be experienced not in the glorious parting of the Red Sea but in the love and forgiveness offered by Jesus on the cross. The true temple of God is no longer to be found in some holy and far away place but is within, as Jesus has made us all temples of the Holy Spirit and in the process challenges us to know God not through mere ritual observance but 'in Spirit and in truth' (Jn 4:23-24).

THE FOURTH SUNDAY OF LENT

First Reading: 2 Chronicles 36:14-16, 19-23

The First and Second Books of Chronicles contain a history of the chosen people beginning with Adam and continuing to the author's own day which is the period following the return of the exiles to Jerusalem and the rebuilding of the temple. Among other things the writer wishes to show that if Israel is faithful to its worship in the temple then their future is secure. In the passage read today, he is outlining the events which led to the disastrous events of the Babylonian exile and explaining that it was the repeated infidelity of the people that brought this situation about. God's plan to form a people for himself, however, would not be thwarted so he used Cyrus the King of Persia to bring the exile to an end and to allow the Jews to return and rebuild their temple. This important event not only showed the faithfulness of God but the re-establishment of the worshipping community in Jerusalem also paved the way for the future coming of the messiah.

Second Reading: Ephesians 2:4-10

The letter to the Ephesians is unlike Paul's other letters in that it is addressed to the whole church and not just to the community at Ephesus. It speaks about Christ in ways that stress his universal significance and highlight the consequences of his death and resurrection for all believers. In this reading, Paul is inviting us to contemplate the staggering generosity of God who has brought us to life in Christ, not because of anything we have done but because of his own mercy. This is pure grace, a gift of God which far exceeds anything we might have hoped for. In bringing us to life in Christ God has created a 'work of art'. We are now capable of living the way God intended us to from the beginning.

Gospel: John 3:14-21

In the synoptic gospels there are three predictions of the passion of Jesus in which he outlines what is going to happen to him when he reaches Jerusalem. This, however, is not the case in John where the passion is prepared for in a completely different way. On three occasions Jesus speaks about himself being 'lifted up'. The Greek word behind this can mean a literal or physical lifting and also an exaltation, a being raised up or glorified. By means of this deliberate play on words the evangelist explains to us that the passion, for all its injustice and brutality, is a glorious revelation of God's love. In this text we have the first prediction of Jesus' death and here the cross is explained as a saving, healing event. Jesus likens his being lifted up (on the cross) to the lifting up of the bronze serpent by Moses in the desert. This is a reference to the occasion when the Israelites had cried out to God to save them from poisonous snakes (Numbers 28). When they looked at the serpent Moses had fashioned from bronze they were healed. So too Jesus, raised up on the cross, is the sign of God's infinite love and the source of our healing.

Reflection

In our day-to-day struggle just to get on with the business of living it is unlikely that we go around with the image of ourselves as 'God's work of art'. There are many forces at work both within us and outside us which tend to pull us down and to leave us with negative feelings about ourselves and those around us. By contrast, at the heart of the gospel message is the wonderful assertion that we are the handiwork of a God who does not make mistakes. This is the God who so loved the world that he gave his only Son not to bully us into obedience or to threaten us with hellfire but to bring us to life in its fullness. This is terrific news indeed, so let us take steps to ensure that other messages do not drown it out.

THE FIFTH SUNDAY OF LENT

First Reading: Jeremiah 31:31-34

Jeremiah is known as the prophet of doom but not by those who are familiar with his message and the context in which he was preaching. He lived during the period leading up to the destruction of Jerusalem and the exile to Babylon (586BC) and he could see the signs of the imminent catastrophe but his warnings fell on deaf ears. Faced with this situation he did not lose himself in despair but rather came to realise that God's faithfulness to Israel could not be undone. In the passage for today the prophet acknowledges that the people's response to the covenant with Moses has been disastrous but such is his faith in God that he can foresee a new day when God will act once more to bring the people to himself. This time it will not be a case of commandments inscribed on tablets of stone. This will be a covenant of the heart whereby everyone will come to know the love of God through an outpouring of his mercy. Even Jeremiah could never have imagined how his prophecy would be fulfilled, that the mercy of God would be shown to one and all through a crucified Christ.

Second Reading: Hebrews 5:7-9
The letter to the Hebrews is one of the most beautiful and yet most difficult books of the New Testament. It was written to Jewish Christians to encourage them to continue to be faithful to Jesus and to understand that he is indeed the fulfilment of all their hopes. One of the greatest difficulties for Jews in accepting Jesus as the messiah was the fact that he died on the cross, apparently rejected by God. The author of the letter to the Hebrews argues that Jesus' death is to be seen as a unique sacrifice of inestimable value which brings to an end all the sacrifices of the temple. In today's text he is referring to Jesus' experience in Gethsemane and he sees in the agony in the garden Jesus coming to an awareness that God was not abandoning him but rather that he would be with him through all the events of his passion. As the Son of God, Jesus teaches us that humility and trust are the virtues which lead to wholeness and holiness.

Gospel: John 12:20-30
The gospel of John is divided into two parts and with this text we approach the end of part one, sometimes known as the Book of Signs. Chapter 12 forms a link between the end of Jesus' public life and the beginning of his passion. The scene is Jerusalem which is full of pilgrims arriving for the feast of Passover. Many of these are Greek-speaking Jews arriving from all around the Roman empire and their request to see Jesus is a reminder that 'seeing' in the fourth gospel is another way of speaking of 'believing in'. On the cross Jesus is drawing all people to himself and inviting a faith response to the love of God that he has manifested. His death is like a seed of grain falling into the ground where it perishes but out of it comes growth and a rich harvest. This is the way of love and all who would follow Jesus must walk this path. By so doing they participate in God's ultimate victory over evil.

Reflection
Jeremiah looked forward to a day when we would all know God, 'the least no less than the greatest'. Some six hundred years later what Jeremiah was speaking about unfolded in the life, death and resurrection of Jesus. With the pilgrims in the gospel

we are invited to say: 'We wish to see Jesus' and to recognise that in the events of Holy Week our request is granted. Now once again Jesus is revealed to us, not as a distant figure from the past who suffered for doing good, but as the living one who even now is calling us to new life. In him we are being offered nothing less than intimate friendship with God. Let us pray with Jesus, 'aloud and in silent tears' that we will be humble enough to accept this transforming gift.

PALM SUNDAY

First Reading: Isaiah 50:4-7
These verses from the Book of the Prophet Isaiah are known as one of the Songs of the Suffering Servant. In fact this is the third song, the others being found in Is 42:1-7, Is 49:1-6 and Is 52:13-53:12. They are grouped together under this heading because they all touch on the theme of suffering which this unknown person must undergo. In its time it was thought that the person was really an embodiment of Israel, the chosen people. However, in the light of the life, death and resurrection of Jesus the early church quickly recognised in these texts predictions of the passion and so it is particularly appropriate that one should be read today on Passion Sunday. We should also note that the fourth song (Is 52) will be read during the liturgy for Good Friday. The theme of the text for today is the servant's confidence in God's presence with him even in the most adverse of circumstances. What sets him apart is the fact that he is, above all, one who listens to God's word and so is strengthened for what lies ahead.

Second Reading: The Letter to the Philipians 2:6-11
Though these beautiful verses are found in Paul's letter to the church at Philippi in northern Greece, it is generally thought that they are part of a hymn which was used in early Christian liturgy and which Paul then placed in his letter because of the relevance of the words. Just before quoting this hymn, Paul is appealing to the community to be more Christ-like in their attitudes and behaviour. He then illustrates that request by highlighting the humility of Jesus who emptied himself of the glory

that was his as the Son of God and came among us as a servant and even went so far as to undergo the agony of the cross. This loving gift of himself then issued in the glory of the resurrection in which God the Father has shown us that Jesus Christ is indeed Lord.

Gospel: Mark 14:1-15:47

The account of the passion in Mark is very stark. Jesus is portrayed as alone, abandoned by his closest friends and perhaps even by God. He dies on the cross with a loud cry on his lips and darkness covers the whole earth. Yet at this precise moment the Roman centurion who was guarding him, having seen how he died, makes the great confession of faith: 'Truly this man was God's Son.' Throughout his ministry Jesus had tried to teach his followers that the way of the kingdom was the way of self emptying love. They had to become servants, slaves to one another and forget about greatness as the world understands it. Repeatedly they failed to understand him and eventually they ran away. So we are left with this foreign outsider to tell us the meaning of Calvary. Through his faithfulness to the kingdom Jesus finally tears away the veil that separates God and suffering humanity. By his prayer of abandonment Jesus has shown us that, far from abandoning us, God has identified totally with our struggle.

Reflection

Suffering is part and parcel of being human and, while we must readily acknowledge this fact, it is also true that we usually do all in our power to avoid it. The readings for today are an invitation to reflect on how it is that passion of Jesus can change our outlook on suffering. Our Saviour may be seen in these texts as a model of patient endurance and of faithfulness. We are not asked to believe that suffering is good in itself but to see that good can come of it and to recognise in Jesus God's solidarity with all those who endure suffering for doing what is right.

The Season of Easter

EASTER SUNDAY

First Reading: Acts 10:34, 37-43

Luke wrote the Acts of the Apostles as a companion volume to his gospel and it has close links to the major themes found there. Just as the gospel story brought us from Galilee to Jerusalem, so the Acts will bring us from Jerusalem to Rome, thus showing the growth of the early church and the acceptance of Jesus by non-Jews. In today's reading we find Peter speaking to a group of Gentiles, the household of the centurion Cornelius, and in his speech he is offering his eyewitness account of the events surrounding the life, death and resurrection of Jesus. These verses highlight for us the central role played by the apostles and early disciples in the spread of the good news. Luke himself only came to faith in Jesus through the witness of others and so in the New Testament there is a strong emphasis on how the first disciples experienced the risen Lord with them. This preaching of the resurrection is the foundation stone on which Christianity rests and Peter, the frightened man who denied even knowing Jesus, now proclaims to anyone who will listen that the risen Lord is the source of forgiveness for all who believe. It is especially significant that Peter the Jew is in a gentile house for in this way he is going beyond what was permitted and is risking defilement by having such contact with non-believers. However, this is one of the fruits of the resurrection – that it breaks down the barriers between peoples.

Second Reading: Colossians 3:1-4

Colossae was a city in the Roman Province of Asia and the letter addressed to the Christian community there by Paul emphasises the consequences of the resurrection of Christ for the whole world and especially for those who have been baptised. As we have already noted, the sacrament of baptism was presented as a sharing in the death of Christ so as to share in the power of his resurrection. This metaphor made sense for those who received baptism through total immersion. Going down into the water was like going into the tomb, it represented death; arising from

45

the water was like entering a new life, the life of the risen Christ. It is this contrast that today's reading is describing. In contrasting 'earthly' and 'heavenly' realities Paul is not asking us to us to ignore or despise our human life on earth. He is stressing that this world can only make sense viewed from a 'heavenly' perspective in other words the perspective of the resurrection.

Gospel: John 20:1-9
This account of the first Easter Sunday morning is significant in that it highlights how each of us as believers must come to terms with the mystery of the resurrection. Mary reports to Peter and the beloved disciple that the tomb is empty. They in turn run to investigate and, while the disciple reaches the tomb first, he holds back in deference to Peter, the leader of the twelve. It is only when the beloved disciple enters the tomb that we are told an appropriate response to the event –'He saw and he believed.' The beloved disciple is unnamed but in John's gospel he is present and close to Jesus at all the key moments: the Last Supper, Calvary and now the tomb. In a sense he symbolises where all true believers should be, for each of us is called to be a beloved disciple who accompanies Jesus on his way: 'Where I am there also my servant will be.' Jn 12:26

Reflection
Our readings today bring home to us with tremendous enthusiasm and fervour how our faith life is meaningless if not rooted in the resurrection of Jesus. The gospel is not merely a story in which we are offered the good example of a man who lived a life of love. It is much more, for it shows us that God has renewed our life totally from within through the Spirit of the Risen Christ who now lives in us. In the world of the New Testament many doubted the resurrection and poured scorn on the idea. The same is true today and perhaps this is not an unreasonable response when confronted with the apparent finality of death. Yet the entire New Testament is a witness to the faith of those who affirmed the resurrection as much more than an historical fact. For them it was the ultimate transforming truth and it remains so for those who celebrate it today. This explains why, 'We are an Easter people and alleluia is our song.' (St Augustine)

THE SECOND SUNDAY OF EASTER

First Reading: Acts of the Apostles 4:32-35
On Easter Sunday we began our reading of extracts from the Acts and this will continue until Pentecost. The texts chosen do not follow a sequence but rather are selected because of the way in which they highlight the spread of the gospel and the transformation which faith in the risen Christ brings about. In the first chapters of Acts, St Luke offers three pen-pictures of the early church and today's reading is the second of these. It stresses that belief in the resurrection bore fruit in the lives of the disciples and brought them together as a community united in faith and love. Their unity showed itself in concrete action as they sought to share all their resources so that no-one was in need. At the centre of this unified community we find the apostles testifying to the power of the resurrection. The witness of the apostles to the presence of the risen Jesus with the community was a cornerstone of the growth of the early church.

Second Reading: 1 John 5:1-6
It is fair to say that Luke offers an idealised picture of the early church for we know from the letters of Paul and John that things did not always go smoothly for the first Christians. The letters of John were written as a kind of commentary on the gospel for it was felt that some people were guilty of misinterpreting its message and undervaluing both the incarnation and the need for brotherly love. In this extract John is stressing once again that the true believer is the one who loves God and God's children, that is the other members of the community. The call to keep God's commandments reminds of Jesus commandment at the last supper in John's gospel: 'Love one another as I have loved you.' We know that this is possible because Jesus shares with us his victory over sin and selfishness. This is a victory achieved by the shedding of his blood and in which we participate through the waters of baptism.

Gospel: John 20:19-31
In this very packed gospel, different facets of the Easter mystery are presented. Firstly we note that Jesus appears to the commu-

nity gathered on a Sunday, they rejoice at his presence and receive through him the gift of the Holy Spirit and with this are given a mission, they are sent just as Jesus himself was. In these verses we have as good a summary of what Sunday Eucharist is all about as we will ever find. In short, it is about joy in the presence of the Risen Lord who give us his peace so that we can continue his task of revealing God to the world. Thankfully Thomas is missing because his refusal to believe means that the following Sunday we need to gather again and once again as a community of faith encounter Christ among us. Now, by a wonderful irony, it is Thomas who leads us in our appropriate response as we acknowledge Jesus as Our Lord and Our God. The words addressed to Thomas by Jesus are for the generations of Christians who have continued to proclaim the Easter message ever since: 'Blessed are those who have not seen and yet believe.'

Reflection
Today's readings originated with different communities at different times in the life of the early church but there is a striking similarity in their insistence that believing in the resurrection heralds a change in the way we live. We simply cannot be true believers if we close our hearts to those in need around us. If we accept the risen Christ and the promise of new life that he brings then we must be engaged in bringing about the kingdom of God. It is not characterised by a private piety but by an inclusive love which reaches out to those who are most in need. Today's gospel gives us John's Pentecost and reminds us that all that we would do in the name of Jesus is to be done in the power of the Holy Spirit.

THE THIRD SUNDAY OF EASTER

First Reading: Acts 3:13-15, 17-19
The context for these words of Peter is the curing of the man who was a cripple from birth. As Peter and John were going into the Temple, the man looked for alms from them but in response to this request he receives a healing. This action causes quite a stir in the Temple precinct and so Peter uses the opportunity to explain to the crowds that they should not be surprised at what

has taken place. It is not by their own power that the apostles have restored this man to health but rather through the power of the risen Jesus at work in them. In his speech to them, Peter stresses three things. Firstly, the continuity between the God of their ancestors and Jesus, whom they crucified; secondly, he apportions no blame to them for his death since they did not know what they were doing. Finally, he calls on them to recognise what has taken place and to repent so that their sins may be forgiven.

Second Reading: 1 John 2:1-5
There are clues in the First Letter of John as to why it may have been written in the first place. They point to the fact that some people in the community are distorting the message of the gospel and the true significance of the death and resurrection of Jesus. In the verses just prior to the ones we read today, John is challenging those who claim to be followers of Jesus yet who are living sinful lives. The problem is made worse by the fact that they refuse to acknowledge that they are sinners. So he writes to remind them that we are all in need of forgiveness and that it comes to us through Jesus who takes away our sins. It appears that there are believers who think that their lifestyle is unimportant as long as they have 'knowledge' about God. They are told that we can be sure we 'know' God only if we are living lives which are consistent with the commandments. Behind this idea of knowledge is the biblical idea of intimacy. It is only by obeying God's word that his love comes to perfection within us.

Gospel: Luke 24:13-35
Only in Luke do we find this resurrection story that is built around the theme of a journey. This is a theme dear to the evangelist as he portrayed Jesus journeying to Jerusalem through the second half of his gospel. Now we are shown disciples coming away from Jerusalem full of disappointment and lacking in understanding. On their journey they are brought to see things differently by a Jesus they only finally recognise at the breaking of bread and in this scene the evangelist invites us to see ourselves. He challenges us with the line 'You foolish people, slow of heart to believe.' These words lie at the centre of the story and explain

what the Emmaus journey is all about. Every Christian must come to a resurrection faith, one that accompanies Jesus through from Good Friday to Easter Sunday. We are invited to understand through our prayerful reading of the scriptures and the events that occur 'on the road' of our lives that the risen Lord still walks with us and meets us, especially when we gather to break bread, that is share in the Eucharist.

Reflection
The first and second readings point to the danger of thinking that just because we belong to what we consider to be the 'true' religion we do not have to concern ourselves with how we live out that faith. Peter is speaking to his fellow-Jews beside the temple in Jerusalem, reminding them of the need for repentance while John is writing to some smug Christians who feel that simply knowing Jesus is enough. The fact is that there must be a connection between what we believe and the way we live. Our faith must show itself in love. The Emmaus story is a reminder that unfortunately, the story of Easter may remain just a retelling of some event from the distant past if we do not allow Jesus to show us how his resurrection is a source of life for us today. Its power is to be experienced in the ordinary events of life as we struggle to be faithful. However, it is often only with hindsight that we can see the ways the Lord has accompanied us on the road.

THE FOURTH SUNDAY OF EASTER

First Reading: Acts 4:8-12
As a result of the healing of the paralytic and the preaching which followed it, Peter and John found themselves arrested by the Temple guards. On the following day they were brought before the Sanhedrin, the ruling council of the Jews, to be questioned about their activities. In the Acts of the Apostles Luke deliberately makes connections between the experience of the early church and what happened to Jesus. The healing of the paralytic is itself a reminder of Jesus' ministry as is the fact that the apostles must now face questions from Caiaphas as did Jesus during his trial. Just as Jesus did everything in the power of the

Spirit, so now Peter likewise stands up to address the assembly 'filled with the Holy Spirit'. His message is brief and to the point. Jesus Christ, raised from the dead, is the one through whom the cripple has been healed and indeed is the only one through whom salvation comes to the whole world.

Second Reading: 1 John 3:1-3
At this point in the letter, it seems that John is almost overwhelmed by the beauty and wonder of what he is describing. He invites his readers to really reflect on just how much God has loved them. Through Jesus they have become children of God, they are united to him in a unique and special way. This is their new-found identity and should be a cause of rejoicing for them. Nor should they be concerned that they are living in a hostile environment. This same world did not acknowledge Jesus' relationship to the Father so then it is not surprising that it does not honour his followers. In addition to being God's children, now they can also look forward to that time when this relationship will come to its full flowering when they are in complete and full union with the Father. At that time they shall see him as he is and so become fully who they are meant to be.

Gospel: John 10:11-18
In the tenth chapter of John's gospel, the focus is on the image of Jesus as the Good Shepherd. This language is to be understood in the light of Old Testament ideas that God was the shepherd of Israel and that their kings were meant to follow his example. Often they failed in this duty and the people were abandoned. It is also to be read in the light of what took place in chapter 9 with the man born blind. The Pharisees in that story represent blind leaders who are incapable of leading the people to God. Jesus, on the other hand, as the Good Shepherd, is the one who lays down his life for his sheep. Not only that, he is aware of them not simply as a flock but he knows each of them individually and they know him. In John, the verb to know has a particular importance because it highlights the fact that coming to faith involves a getting to know Jesus, it is all about a personal relationship. Each of us is invited to come to know the one who lays down his life for us in act of love.

Reflection

In this time between Easter and Pentecost we might be tempted to think of these events as historical moments in the distant past which gave rise to the religion which we practice today. This religion for many is then seen as a moral code by which they live in the hope of attaining heaven. For Peter and John, however, the Christian experience was something very much in the here and now. They felt that their lives were driven by the Spirit of Jesus which made them aware on a daily basis of how God was at work in the world and in their own hearts. These readings are a powerful witness to the terrific dynamism which characterises a genuine Christianity. If it seems too far removed from our experience perhaps it is a sign that we need to invite the Holy Spirit to reawaken in us the joyful energy which comes from understanding the love that the Father has lavished on us. We are challenged to come to know Jesus as our Good Shepherd who even now leads us to restful waters and gives us repose.

THE FIFTH SUNDAY OF EASTER

First Reading: Acts 9:26-31

Chapter 9 of Acts gives the first account of the conversion of St Paul on his way to Damascus. There are two other accounts of it in the Acts of the Apostles. In this reading we hear of some of the fallout from that dramatic event, especially as it affected the church in Jerusalem. Paul, or Saul as he was still known, was smuggled out of Damascus because of a plot to kill him and, having made his way to Jerusalem to speak to the leaders of the community, he found that he was met with considerable suspicion and fear. Barnabas, however, an important member of the community, first mentioned in Acts 4:36, brought him to the apostles and explained to them all about his conversion. After this he took part in the work of the church in Jerusalem, but once again encountered the wrath of some Jews. This time it was Hellenists, that is to say, Greek speaking Jews, who were determined to get rid of him. So he was removed from the scene and sent back to his home place, Tarsus. St Luke tells us that after the upheavals caused both by Saul's persecution and then his conversion, things settled down for the communities which existed throughout Palestine.

Second Reading: 1 John 3:18-24

In this reading we return once again to themes which are central to the letter, namely the need for a life which is consistent with what we believe and an awareness that we are called to union with God. Since we are children of the truth then our love must show itself in practical deeds and not be just talk. This in turn gives us confidence to come before God to ask him for what we need. God will answer our prayers because we are keeping the commandments and for John these can be reduced to two: that we believe in Jesus and that we love one another as he told us to. To live out our lives in this way means that we are living in God and he is living in us. We can know that God is living in us by the Spirit that he has given us. This important theme is put before us as we move towards the feast of Pentecost.

Gospel: John 15:1-8

This Sunday in our reading from John there is a change in symbolism from shepherding to that of the vine. This too is an image that derives from the Old Testament where the prophets speak of the chosen people as God's vine that he tends with love in the hope of it producing choice fruit. The evangelist now takes that same idea and revolutionises it by showing us that Jesus is the true vine and the disciples are his branches, in other words they cannot and do not exist apart from him. Two important aspects of the believer's relationship with Jesus emerge from this: intimacy and fruitfulness. We are in complete union with him, that is, we remain or abide in him and draw life from him. Since we draw life from him then we will bear fruit and that means that we cannot claim to be his disciples and live only for ourselves.

Reflection

Looking at the story of Paul in the first reading, we are reminded that we can never predict how and where God will speak to us. It is not difficult to imagine the fear of the Jerusalem church when they heard that Saul was back from Damascus. Some of them had probably witnessed his involvement in the death of Stephen, and now they were being asked to believe that he had become one of them. Surely it was a trick! It took Barnabas to show them the way. Just as God was to be found in a crucified

Messiah, why couldn't he now be working through Saul the Pharisee? Sometimes faith demands that we take risks because God would have us look for him in the most unexpected places. If we are attached to Jesus the true vine, then our faith will be nourished and we will remain in him.

THE SIXTH SUNDAY OF EASTER

First Reading: Acts 10:25-26, 34-35, 44-48
For a full appreciation of what is taking place in this story, it would be helpful to read all of chapter 10. This incident marks a very important turning point for Peter and indeed for the whole church. Cornelius is a Roman centurion who, even though he is sympathetic to the Jewish religion, is still regarded as a gentile and therefore unclean. In a vision he has been told to send for Simon Peter whom he does not yet know. For his part, Peter has also had a vision in which he sees God telling him to eat unclean food. The two men are brought together and it becomes a moment of great grace for both of them. Peter learns that the good news of Jesus must be preached to everyone and that he can no longer consider Gentiles as in any way inferior. Cornelius learns that the God of the Jewish religion which he has admired for so long is now reaching out to him through the Spirit of his Son Jesus. The Gentiles receive the Holy Spirit and the Jews who are present are astounded at this development.

Second Reading: 1 John 4:7-10
With these few words we come to perhaps the best summary of what Christianity is all about. John returns to the theme of love as the core commandment. However, this commandment is not something which has simply been imposed from on high; rather it issues from the very nature of God who is love, who acts in love and who sent his Son to reveal the fullness of that love. God has loved us first and in the self-sacrifice of Jesus we see what that means. He has opened up for us the possibility of truly loving God and one another. Jesus doesn't simply give us good example as to how we should behave, he actually empowers us to do as he did. By this means we are drawn into the very life of God and are made new.

54

Gospel: John 15:9-17

These verses continue the text from last Sunday and tease out the implications of the vine symbolism and what it means to abide or remain in Jesus. The underlying reasoning is simply this: everything arises out of the loving relationship between Jesus and the Father. Throughout his life Jesus is responding to the Father's love and making it known. As the disciples come to faith in Jesus they are being drawn into that loving relationship and they too can share the joy that enthuses Jesus and inspires him to reveal his Father to the world. The one sure way of knowing that their faith is true is their love for one another. Just as Jesus was prepared to lay down his life for them, so too must they be willing to live in humble service of one another.

Reflection

The gospel and letters of John were probably written around 100 AD and were among the last parts of the New Testament to be penned. It is as though the prayer and reflection of the first generations of believers finally brought them to an understanding of what the whole Christian experience was all about and it could be summed up in three simple words: *God is Love*. This is neither pious sentimentality nor a bland cliché for, if it is taken seriously, nothing can ever be the same again. Peter and Cornelius both discovered that this is a love that makes changes and shatters old certainties. This is the love which proves that God will stop at nothing to convince a weak and wounded humanity of its immeasurable worth and dignity. The sad thing is that we often still choose to live in the darkness surrounded by our prejudice and fear. Or worse still, we imagine that being a follower of Jesus is about intellectual adherence to dogmas rather than a living out of a relationship of love.

THE ASCENSION OF THE LORD

First Reading: Acts1:1-11

St Luke is the only one of the evangelists to write a companion to his gospel and it serves the purpose of showing the transition between the ministry of Jesus and the mission of the church. In this reading from the opening verses of the Acts of the Apostles

Luke addresses Theophilus, the man for whom he wrote and explains how events unfolded after the resurrection. The risen Lord appeared to the apostles on many occasions and pointed out to them that the resurrection does not herald the end of time but marks the beginning of their mission for they will soon have to be his witnesses throughout the world. They can only be effective witnesses when the Holy Spirit empowers them, so they must now await the outpouring of the Spirit. In preparing for his departure in this way, the ascension is portrayed not so much as a leave-taking but as a necessary next step in the unfolding drama of our salvation. This explains why there is no lengthy description of the ascension and the importance of the men in white who urge the apostles not to stand looking up into the sky. So they return to Jerusalem and devote themselves to prayer as they await the day of Pentecost.

Second Reading: Ephesians 4:1-13
In the letter to the Ephesians Paul, who is in prison, writes to the community to remind them of the importance of living in a way which reflects the importance of their calling. Such a lifestyle will be characterised by a loving service of one another and a desire to remain united in the faith. This is because when Christ ascended into heaven it was to send forth the Spirit which sums up all the gifts of God. Each member of the church has received the Holy Spirit through baptism and so each one has a role to play in the community. By faithfully playing out that role the church becomes more fully what it is meant to be, the Body of Christ. For Paul the ascension highlights the fact that Jesus first descended and removed all the barriers that separated humanity from God.

Gospel: Mark 16:15-20
These remarkable verses are taken from what is sometimes called the longer ending of Mark's gospel and they represent a final summary explanation of the meaning of Jesus' life, death and resurrection. Mark offers no description of the ascension of the Lord but sees the whole mystery in the light of Easter. It is the good news that all who respond to Jesus in faith are saved and the power of the risen Christ will be with the church to en-

sure the success of its mission. The signs that are mentioned are not to be taken literally but show that, in Jesus, good triumphs and evil is defeated. The affirmation that those who do not believe will be condemned is not understood by the church as saying that only Christians will get into heaven. Rather it is a warning about those who willfully refuse to respond to God at work in their life. Christians are always asked to leave judgement to God.

Reflection

It is a temptation for every generation of Christians to stand looking up to heaven and wringing their hands wishing that Jesus walked our streets as he did the streets of Palestine or that he would come back in some dramatic way to show the world the error of its ways. However, such an attitude entirely fails to appreciate the dignity of our calling. We have been entrusted with a task and today's feast is a reminder to us that Jesus only left this world so that he could be with us in a more effective way. So, in the coming week let us pray with urgency for a renewed outpouring of the Spirit so that we can become more effective witnesses of his love.

PENTECOST SUNDAY

First Reading: Acts 2:1-11

The feast of Pentecost was originally a Jewish feast celebrated fifty days after Passover (the word *pentecost* means fifty in Greek). On this day they recalled the giving of the Law to Moses on Mount Sinai and with that the birth of the Jewish people who were bound to their God by this covenant. It is, therefore, a very appropriate day to remember the gift of the Holy Spirit being given to the apostles, for the new people of God now live not by the Law but by the Spirit of God. St Luke is the only person in the New Testament to describe the events of this day and he brings to the fore the symbols which point to the presence of the Spirit. Firstly, the apostles hear the sound of a mighty wind and in the Old Testament the Spirit is the breath of God which 'blows where it wills' (John 3:8). The Spirit then takes the form of tongues of fire, a reminder of a Jewish tradition which said that on Mt Sinai when God spoke, his word divided into 70 tongues. At that time this was believed to be the number of nations in the world. Now the Spirit comes upon each person present and with this gift they are able to speak the languages of the world. All those who hear them understand them in their own tongue and, as St Luke tells us, there were pilgrims from all over the world gathered for the feast. The barrier of language between different peoples is removed as the whole community hears the wonders that God has done being proclaimed. The atmosphere is one of an exuberant and joyful new beginning.

Second Reading: Galatians 5:16-25
In this letter, Paul was writing to one of the Christian communities which he had founded who had recently come under the influence of some Jewish Christians. These people were trying to make them observe the precepts of the Law of Moses and so Paul immediately reminded them that they were not to be guided by the Law but by the Spirit of Jesus. It was the presence of this Spirit in them that would guarantee that they lived the true Christian life. If they were attuned to the gift of the Spirit, which was theirs through baptism, then the fruits of the Spirit would become evident in how they lived. In order to drive the point home Paul contrasts the consequences of a life of self-indulgence with what the Spirit brings.

Gospel: John 15:26-27, 16:12-15
The fourth gospel speaks of the Holy Spirit as the Paraclete or Advocate. The word is taken from legal language and may refer to a lawyer for the defence, but it also means a guide and today's text, taken from two different chapters of John, speaks to us about both aspects. The work of the Holy Spirit is to makes us confident witnesses as we show the world that there is more to life that mere survival or the pursuit of pleasure. The Spirit of truth allows us to witness in every era to the timeless message of God's love – a truth revealed in the life, death and resurrection of Jesus. However, such is the depth of the mystery of the Word made flesh that no single generation can grasp it entirely and so we are guided by the Spirit in coming to a greater understanding of what is revealed

Reflection

Birthdays deserve to be celebrated. They are occasions when we can be thankful for the gift of life, and for the love we have received. They provide the opportunity for families to get together and recall good memories from the past and also a chance to look to the future, aware of how far we have come. So it is with Pentecost. Today is the birthday of the church, a time for us to celebrate who we are and to rediscover what it means to be the people of God. Down through the centuries the Holy Spirit has guided the church, despite the weaknesses of its members, both clerical and lay. We have the witness of many generous and heroic people who have been 'led by the Spirit' and whose lives have given eloquent testimony to the power of God at work in them. Today, then, let's take heart and invoke the Spirit of God that we may be filled with a joyful appreciation of who we are and what we have to give. This brings with it many challenges, since for many religious people their faith acts as a sort of security blanket, offering certainty and security. However, the good news is not about how things were in the past but about the Spirit of God at work now and always.

Feasts of the Lord in Ordinary Time.

Trinity Sunday and the Feast of the Body and Blood of the Lord are celebrated in Ordinary Time on the two Sundays following Pentcost.

TRINITY SUNDAY

First Reading: Deuteronomy 4:32-34, 39-40
There is no reference to the Holy Trinity in the Old Testament, as this understanding of the nature of God could only come about through the person of Jesus. However, the Old Testament prepares the way for that by its insistence on the uniqueness of Israel's God and the special relationship which that God forged with his people throughout their history. Today's reading highlights that unique bond between God and the Israelites by asking has there ever been anything quite like this before? Has any God ever sought to make himself known in such a way or called a people to himself by a covenant which is rooted in their own history of liberation from slavery? Deuteronomy is written in the form of Moses' last will and testament. Their great leader is reminding the people before they enter the promised land of all that God has done for them and he is calling on them to live in a way which reflects the truth about their God.

Second Reading: Romans 8:14-17
If the idea of the Trinity, three persons in one God, seems too much of a mystery to contemplate then perhaps a reading such as this can help us to come to some appreciation of the remarkable truth which Jesus has revealed. In this part of the letter to the Romans, Paul is explaining how the Christian life is one that is made totally new by our being drawn into the very life of God. The Spirit of Jesus which we have received through baptism means that we have a share in the relationship which Jesus has with his Father. As Jesus called out to God in his moment of anguish 'Abba' (an Aramaic word meaning Daddy) so too we, who have been made children of God, can call out in the same way. Jesus the Son has the revealed the love of the Father and we live in that love through the Spirit we have been given.

Gospel: Matthew 28:16-18

These are the closing verses of the gospel of Matthew and they illustrate very well the growing faith of the early church in what Jesus has revealed. The life, death and resurrection of Jesus witness to the activity of God the Father through him, and now at the end of the gospel we see Jesus not leaving his disciples but promising to be with them until the end of time as they fulfil their mission of making disciples of all nations by baptising them and teaching them to observe his commands. This text is ideal for today as it is a reminder that faith in the Trinity brings with it a mission to let the whole world hear the good news about God.

Reflection

It is a striking fact that in the ancient world those civilisations that were great in terms of conquest, building, literature and philosophy have left us little or nothing of their religious beliefs. On the other hand, a people who were considered of no particular significance from a small stretch of land in the eastern Mediterranean have passed on to us their enduring concept of God. This is not a god of pagan superstition nor even of the philosophers. This is Yahweh, the God of Israel, who became known to the people through the experience of their own history and who subsequently revealed himself in Jesus of Nazareth. Today we are not celebrating a mystery we are never destined to understand; rather we are contemplating the God in whose image we are made and whose name is Love.

THE FEAST OF THE BODY AND BLOOD OF CHRIST

First Reading: Ex 24:3-8

The Book of Exodus tells the story of the single most important event in the history of the chosen people. It relates how the Israelites were saved from slavery in Egypt and brought out to Mount Sinai where God bound himself to them in a covenant. In the ancient world covenants were formal agreements in which the parties were obliged to stand by the promises made to each other. In Exodus, God's action in freeing the Israelites from oppression is the first step in this covenant and Moses' reception of

61

the commandments on Mt Sinai is the next phase. In today's reading we are told how Moses instructs the people to enter into the covenant through an ancient ceremony of ratification. Blood is the symbol of life and the sprinkling of the blood of the animals signifies the people's desire to participate in the relationship as outlined in the book of the Law. The symbolism of this act will be brought to an entirely different level by the sacrifice of Jesus on the cross.

Second Reading: Hebrews 9:11-15
Hebrews is one of the most difficult writings in the New Testament. This is because it was written to explain to Jewish Christians just how the death of Jesus on the cross marked the end of the temple liturgy with its emphasis on the sacrifice of animals for the purification of sins. Since we are not familiar with the traditions of the temple it can be hard for us to appreciate the staggering claims which the author is making. He argues that Jesus is both the priest offering the sacrifice and the victim being offered. In so doing, he brings to God the perfect sacrifice which takes away our sins in a way never imagined before. In Jesus, God has done for us what we could not do for ourselves and in the Eucharist we have been left a memorial of this action. As the covenant on Mt Sinai was marked by a meal, so now the new covenant is celebrated by a meal. In this meal we share in Christ's self offering through continuing to do as he commanded us at the last supper.

Gospel: Mark 14:12-16, 22-26
The last supper accounts in the gospels can only be properly understood against the background of the Jewish Feast of Passover. At the time of Jesus Jews all over the Roman Empire gathered to celebrate this great feast, seeing in it not only a glorious past event but also the promise of a new intervention by God when he would once again act to free them from oppression and remove the guilt of their sin. It is precisely this understanding that we find in today's reading from Mark. Jesus' action at the table is a ritual that anticipates his life-giving death. His death on the cross inaugurates a new covenant, a new relationship between God and his people. This is why it is so

important for us to 'do this in memory' of him. As the new people of God we celebrate our identity when we come together for Eucharist. We give thanks for who we are and all that God has done for us.

Reflection

To understand the Eucharist we do not need to be experts in theology nor in the rituals of ancient Israel. Jesus left us the symbols of bread and wine as realities that speak to us of nourishment and celebration. He gave us these realities the night before he died as he shared a meal with his dearest friends in the world. As on the next day he would give his life on the cross, so in this meal he gave himself to them, a lasting gift of love and friendship that only God could give. By participating in it we commit ourselves to the new and everlasting covenant, a covenant which recognises that we are brothers and sisters of Jesus and children of the one Father. As we share the meal let us pray for the grace to live a life that is worthy of it.

Ordinary Time

FIRST SUNDAY IN ORDINARY TIME – THE BAPTISM OF THE LORD

First Reading: Is 55:1-11

This impassioned plea for people to become aware of their hunger and thirst for the things of God is a very appropriate text for the first Sunday in Ordinary time. Having celebrated Advent and Christmas we settle down now to reflecting on the marvellous mystery that was revealed in the public life of Jesus and in this text from Isaiah we get a glimpse of the type of scripture that inspired Jesus as he set out to be faithful to his Father's will. Here we read that God is indeed faithful and generous and that only in him can the human heart be truly nourished. The prophet invites people to search for God, certain in the knowledge that, in him, they will find a healing welcome. In the Old Testament it becomes clear that the word of God is not about ordinary speech or even text in a holy book but rather refers to the effective and fruitful revelation of God's saving will. This is what the prophets proclaimed and what Jesus will bring to fulfilment.

Second Reading: 1 John 5:1-9

The letters of John were probably written after his gospel in an effort to correct some misinterpretations that were circulating at the time (ca 95-100AD). It seems that some were arguing that the gospel of John played down the importance of Jesus' humanity and the relevance of his death on the cross and now the author wishes to make it clear that believing in Jesus involves accepting his life-giving death. This means understanding that the blood and water that flowed from his side are symbols of baptism and Eucharist which give life to all believers. This is the work of the Holy Spirit and we are not true disciples of Jesus if we do not live according to this insight, recognising that through our baptism we share in his victory over sin and death.

Gospel: Mark 1:7-11

In all the gospels the baptism of Jesus marks the beginning of his public ministry and the focus is on Jesus' identity as he sets out to proclaim the kingdom of God. In Mark's account of the event it is clear that what takes place is for Jesus' sake, as we are told that it is he (and not the crowds) who sees the Spirit descend in the form of the dove and the voice from heaven is addressed to him as it proclaims: 'You are my beloved Son.' The evangelist would have us understand that, as Jesus sets out on his mission, he does with a sense of who he is before God. It is precisely this that allows him to be faithful to his task to the very end.

Reflection

Today's feast is an invitation to reflect on our own baptism. We too have been baptised with the Holy Spirit, the same Spirit that empowered Jesus to proclaim the kingdom and to endure the sufferings that lay before him. In our baptism the Spirit proclaims to each of us that we are God's beloved and challenges us to be true to ourselves and to our God as we try to live according to the values of the kingdom that Jesus preached.

THE SECOND SUNDAY IN ORDINARY TIME

First Reading: 1 Samuel 3:3-10, 19

This reading tells the delightful story of the call of the boy Samuel who was living at the shrine of the Lord in Shiloh. His mother Hannah, who had been barren and who had pleaded with the Lord for the gift of a son, had dedicated him to God from his birth. Now we see the beginning of his close relationship to God as he is called to be a judge in Israel and to lead his people through some very difficult times. We are told that the boy did not recognise the voice of God calling him since he had no knowledge of God, and indeed that the old priest Eli also failed to understand what was happening at first. However, on the third occasion when God calls, Eli explains to the boy what he must say, using words which express a total surrender in faith: 'Speak, Lord, your servant is listening.' Such openness meant that for the rest of his life God was with him and he, in turn, was dedicated to proclaiming God's word in season and out of season.

Second Reading: 1 Corinthians 6:13-15, 17-20

In chapterss 5 and 6 of this letter, Paul is dealing with certain moral questions which have emerged for the community, and in the section being read today he is challenging those people who believe that sexuality is a morally indifferent area. Their thinking was based on the idea that the body and everything physical was inferior to the soul and everything spiritual and so it didn't really matter what one did in the body. Paul rejects this pagan thinking which tried to separate the body and soul and emphasises that body and soul we are meant for the Lord. This means that sexual immorality is a sin against our own body which is a temple of the Spirit and also a sin against the body of Christ which is the community. For Paul, Christian morality was not simply a commandment handed down from on high; rather the moral life grows out of and is consequence of our belonging to Christ.

Gospel: John 1:35-42

The gospel of John offers a different perspective when it comes to certain aspects of Jesus' life and the response he evokes. This is very clear in today's gospel text which tells of the call of the first disciples. In the other gospels, Jesus simply says 'Follow me' and they do (see next Sunday). John, however, describes something of a process whereby firstly they come to know something of Jesus through the word of the Baptist who calls him the Lamb of God. They follow behind Jesus, interested to know where he lives and Jesus in turn invites them to 'Come and see.' As the fourth gospel progresses it becomes clear that this invitation is actually a call to discipleship, to embark on a journey of faith during which they will come to a greater understanding of who Jesus is and what it means to be with him. This becomes very clear in the stories of the Samaritan Woman (chapter 4) and the Man born Blind (chapter 9) where each of them is brought gradually to a point of recognition and faith.

Reflection

The idea of a relationship of trusting faithfulness underlies the notion of faith in the Bible, and everything else including our morality flows from this. We can learn a great deal from both

Samuel and Paul about a morality based on the scriptures. For these men, all their actions arose out of their relationship with God. This was the determining factor when they asked themselves the question 'What should I do?' If today many people fail to understand the demands of a Christian morality, could it be that like the boy Samuel they 'have as yet no knowledge of the Lord'? If our approach to morality is based solely on our own wants and needs, then Paul's statement that 'You are not your own property, you have been bought and paid for' will make no sense to us. Christian living is really only possible when we have come to know Christ and have responded to the invitation to 'Come and see.'

THE THIRD SUNDAY IN ORDINARY TIME

First Reading: Jonah 3:1-5, 10
While Jonah is numbered among the prophets, the book which bears his name is in fact a parable and is quite unlike the writings of the other prophets. The central character is called by God to preach to the Assyrian people in their capital city Nineveh. The Assyrians were the Israelites' worst enemies and there is much evidence for their barbaric cruelty. So outrageous is this request that Jonah decides to escape in the opposite direction. Such efforts are, of course, futile and he ends up doing what he was asked to do. As we see from today's reading, the Ninevites repent when they hear his preaching, much to Jonah's annoyance, for he would have preferred that they be destroyed with fire and brimstone by an angry God. The significance of this parable is that it was written at a time when the chosen people were striving to cut themselves off from all others by emphasising their ethnic and moral superiority. The message of the parable is that we are all God's children and we are all in need of repentance if we are going to come to knowledge of the true God.

Second Reading: 1 Corinthians 7:29-31
In chapter 7 of the letter, Paul is dealing with questions relating to lifestyle and in particular whether one should opt for the married or celibate state, and it is in this context that today's reading is to be understood. Paul's answer is that the important thing is

not whether a person is married or celibate but how we live out our particular choice. His belief that the second coming of Christ would be soon colours his outlook concerning all human activity and relationships. This is why in today's reading he appears to give such unusual advice to the community. However, we can still draw a very relevant message from his teaching and that is that we should always live with the awareness that 'the world as we know it is passing away'. Such an outlook allows us to focus on the values of the kingdom of God rather than those of the marketplace.

Gospel: Mark 1:14-20

With this gospel we have the beginning of the proclamation of the good news in Mark. Jesus is portrayed as discerning that the time is right for people to respond to the preaching of the kingdom. The essence of his message is simple: it is time to repent and believe. Behind the word to repent there is a much stronger meaning than simply 'Be sorry and start again.' Rather Jesus is looking for *conversion*, a change of mindset and attitude that will leave us open to God and allow us to trust that the news really is good. The radical response of the two sets of brothers shows something of what is intended, they leave their nets and they follow. The road they are taking will bring them to places they never imagined and will show them that following Jesus is a constant challenge to put themselves entirely into God's hands.

Reflection

Both readings today warn us about the dangers of being self-obsessed. The parable of Jonah speaks very clearly of the dangers involved in imagining that we are better than everyone else. Such an attitude blinds us both to the goodness in others and the graciousness of our God whose mercy reaches out to all. Paul is trying to get across to groups, who are trying to outdo each other in terms of their Christian virtue, that they don't have to go making radical changes to their lifestyle in order to be faithful to the gospel. It is much more important that in the ordinary details of their daily life and relationships they are guided by the love of Christ.

The Fourth Sunday in Ordinary Time

First Reading: Deuteronomy 18:15-20
Deuteronomy is the fifth and last book of the Torah (also known as the Pentateuch), and is presented as the last will and testament of Moses who is about to die just before the chosen people enter the Promised Land. The book was written centuries after the events described in it took place and it was intended to act as a force for renewal in the living out of the covenant in the conditions which prevailed long after the Israelites had settled in the land. In today's text, the people are reminded that just as God has blessed them with a great prophet like Moses in the past so too he would raise up others who would speak the word of the Lord to them. They had to be wary, however, of false prophets and those who would lead them astray. The full significance of the text is to be seen in the gospel for today when Jesus appears as the new Moses who would speak the word of God in an even more authoritative way.

The Second Reading: 1 Corinthians 7:32-35
With this reading we are still dealing with the situation which was addressed last week. Since Paul is convinced that the world as we know it is coming to an end he views the life-long commitment of marriage as perhaps a more difficult choice in relation to preparing oneself for the end. So here he is speaking not to people who are already married but to those who are deciding about their future. Given that the second coming did not take place and that the church later recognised in marriage a sacrament of God's presence, it would be a grave mistake to take this reading as in any way undervaluing the married state.

Gospel: Mark 1:21-28
A dominant aspect of Jesus' work in proclaiming the good news of the kingdom in Mark is his role as a teacher and this is particularly evident in the early chapters. Here we see his teaching making a deep impression on his hearers and they respond with wonder and astonishment. In this teaching Jesus was, no doubt, speaking of God's will for the world in terms that were easily understood by his hearers. Added to this, his action of exorcis-

ing demons can be understood as a way of indicating the triumph of good over evil and showing that now is the time to respond with faith to God's action in the world. The prevalence of exorcisms in the gospels is not to be taken as suggesting there was more demonic possession then than now. It is more likely that these accounts reflect ancient views around a range of illnesses that are more easily diagnosed nowadays.

Reflection

In this age of information technology and instant access to information and entertainment, we probably appreciate more than ever the worth of a really good teacher. It is an aspect of Jesus' ministry that can easily be lost sight of, and that is a pity because it is more important that we understand his message than that we believe he was a miracle worker. As disciples we are challenged to continue to grow in understanding, to sit at the feet of Jesus the teacher and to take steps to make our own the wonderful good news of the kingdom. By being properly informed, we are less likely to be led astray by the whole range of 'false prophets' who today compete for our allegiance.

THE FIFTH SUNDAY IN ORDINARY TIME

First Reading: Job 7:1-4, 6-7

'Why do people suffer?' is a question that has engaged the greatest religious and philosophical minds throughout history. One such person is the writer of the book of Job who wrote his masterpiece sometime in the fifth century BC. This work tells the story of the perfect man who, even though he only does good and is recognised by God as just, still suffers terribly. Initially he responds with patience to his plight but he soon turns to question the God who would allow such things to happen. The verses we read today sum up very powerfully the dilemma in which he finds himself. His life seems meaningless and there is no end in sight to the misery he endures. This text is chosen in order to highlight the difference Jesus makes and that is clearly shown in the gospel for today when all those afflicted by illness and suffering seek him out in order to find healing and peace. However, in its own time the book of Job played a very important role in challenging the widely accepted view that the good were always blessed and the wicked punished. This led to the presumption that if something bad happened to a person it was a direct punishment from God for sin. The book of Job, in addressing the problem, does not explain the meaning of suffering but at least it lays to rest the notion that suffering is somehow always a punishment.

Second Reading 1 Corinthians 9:16-19, 22-23
Some people in the community in Corinth made much of the freedom that their faith in Christ brought them, but Paul is at pains to show them that the gospel message does not only bring 'freedom from' but also 'freedom for'. We have been made free from selfishness in order to serve others and that is exactly what Paul is doing. In Corinth Paul worked and paid his own way so as not to be a burden on the community. Some had challenged him on this, saying that a 'real' apostle would not do this and in chapter 9 of the letter we read his defence against the charge. For Paul the bottom line is simply this: that Christ be known and loved and he will do whatever it takes so that everyone may come to an awareness of the good news, irrespective of social class or ethnic background.

Gospel: Mark 1:29-39
We continue reading from the first chapter of Mark and its emphasis on Jesus as the one who inaugurates the kingdom of God. Now it is his healing ministry that highlights God's triumph over the powers of darkness. This is dramatically symbolised in the fact that it is after sunset on the Sabbath that the people come crowding around the door. During the Sabbath they were not allowed to bring their loved ones to him as this would be considered work, but now they flock to him in search of his healing compassion. As before, Jesus does not permit the demons to speak and here an important theme of the gospel is being alluded to. People have definite expectations of what a Messiah should be, and what Jesus is offering will be different and so he refuses to allow a mistaken notion of his purpose to develop. Rather he commits himself to his task by taking time out to pray alone and then continuing his mission of proclaiming the kingdom.

Reflection

The friends who came to comfort Job in his suffering were no comfort at all because they only offered him platitudes derived from poor doctrine. Job, for his part, insisted there must be more to God than what he was being told and it was this determination to really know God that brought him to the experience outlined in the final chapters of the book (38-42). Sometimes, in order to feel secure and certain, religious people can speak of God in ways which are only a demonstration of their ignorance and fear. As Jesus showed, God will be better known through love in action than through any statement of doctrine.

THE SIXTH SUNDAY IN ORDINARY TIME

Leviticus 13:1-2, 44-46

The Book of Leviticus is concerned with laws, especially those governing the practice of worship in the temple. It belongs to what is known as the priestly source of Old Testament writing, that is, the material which the Jerusalem priests were responsible for editing. The extract read today deals with the law concerning people afflicted with a contagious skin disease that is usually translated as leprosy. Experts believe that the disease referred to here is not leprosy as we know it today, but whatever is referred to caused fear and loathing in the community. The victims had to be driven out of the community as long as they showed the symptoms and could only be readmitted when they had been recognised as cured by the priest. In some places in the Bible leprosy is given as a punishment for sin and such stories no doubt added to the sense of disgust which is associated with this condition. Why then are we reading such a text? The answer is to be seen in the gospel for today, where Jesus' ministry, instead of driving people out of the community, seeks to include them. His response to this affliction is compassion.

Second Reading: 1 Corinthians 10:31-11:1

These verses represent the conclusion to a discussion which has taken place in chapters 8-10 and concerns the question of whether Christians should eat meat that had been offered to idols in pagan temples. While this may seem a long way removed from modern concerns, Paul's treatment of the problem offers an important lesson for all Christians. Some in the community argued that since idols had no existence in reality then eating meat that had been sacrificed to them was not an issue, it was just meat. Paul accepted the theory but he went on to point out that some in the community were not as strong in their faith and were being scandalised by this behaviour. So he argued that for the sake of charity and out of concern for others, they should perhaps abstain from this practice. His reasoning is summed up in the short extract we read today. As believers in Jesus we must always strive to be sensitive to others and not to simply rely on being right all the time.

Gospel: Mark 1:40-45

In the New Testament the healing ministry of Jesus does not focus so much on his ability to heal as on what the healings mean. This is particularly clear in today's incident. The leper who comes to Jesus is not only suffering because of his physical condition, he is also excluded from his community in the manner outlined in the first reading. This clearly adds to his sense of isolation and abandonment. So when he begs for healing, Jesus is moved with compassion at the sight of his suffering. In healing him, however, he also insists that he take the steps required to be readmitted to the community. In this way, this miracle of Jesus touches not only the victim but also all those around him. Jesus is not only healing the leprosy, he is also challenging attitudes to it and this is made obvious when he reaches out and touches the leper.

Reflection

There are many examples from religious traditions around the world, including Christianity, which show that religion is often used as a means of excluding people or as a way of creating an elite or perfect group. However, it is clear both from what Jesus said and what he did that the kingdom of God is inclusive. He reached out to those who were deemed rejected by God and even went so far as to include himself among them when he went to the cross. Let us strive to recognise and overcome our own intolerance and to replace it with the compassion of Christ.

THE SEVENTH SUNDAY IN ORDINARY TIME

First Reading: Isaiah 43:18-19, 21-22, 24-25
As we have noted before, chapters 40-55 of Isaiah date from the period towards the end of the exile of the Israelites in Babylon (ca 540) and the prophet writes to console the people with hope for a new future. Previously much of the teaching of prophets centred on exhorting their hearers to remember what God had done for them in the past, especially in the great event of the exodus and their journey through the desert to the promised land. This was the proof of God's saving love for them and from it they could renew their faith and trust in the Lord. Now, however, the prophet boldly announces that there is no need to think about the past, nor to recall past glories for God is about to do a new thing. They are going to travel through the wilderness once again but this time they are going home to Jerusalem and they will learn once again to sing the praises of God. All this is possible because God has chosen to obliterate the memory of the sins that led to their downfall. He is now revealed, not simply as the just God of the covenant, but as their merciful Lord.

Second Reading: 2 Corinthians 1:18-22
Paul's second letter to the community in Corinth continues to give insight into his stormy relationship with some of the people there. As we know, the first letter addressed some of the problems which had arisen because of faction fighting among different groups. In this letter it is not always easy to work out exactly what the new difficulties are but it is clear that Paul feels the need to defend himself as an apostle and the authenticity of his message. From chapter 1:15-17 it is clear that Paul has changed his travel plans and will not now be visiting the community. This change has led to the charge that he is inconsistent and just suiting himself, so he replies to that accusation by an appeal to his preaching about Jesus. He never wavered or vacillated in proclaiming the good news that Jesus is God's *yes* to humanity. In him, all God's promises all fulfilled. Everything that Paul does is rooted in that conviction and so he is not persuaded to change his plans for purely human reasons.

Gospel: Mark 2:1-12

In chapter one of Mark's gospel it was very evident how Jesus' proclamation of the kingdom was accomplished in both word and deed. He taught in the synagogues and he healed and performed exorcisms wherever he found people suffering. By his preaching and his actions Jesus was pointing to the presence of God in their midst and in today's incident he does so again, this time through the gift of forgiveness. The scene invites reflection as Jesus' action not only frees this man from the paralysis of sin but also highlights the obstacles Jesus has to face from those who seek the limit the ways in which God's mercy may be experienced. It is interesting to note that the spark for Jesus' action is the faith of those who go to such trouble to bring their friend to him and that the response of the crowds is once again wonder and praise.

Reflection

A cynical commentator on religion once paraphrased the scriptures with the words: 'In the beginning was the Word and the word was No!' This is profoundly sad because, as we can see from these readings, God's word to us yesterday, today and forever is always Yes. He says yes to life, to love and to everything that is good for humanity, for God only wants to show us how to avoid the path to self-destruction and to how find our true home in him. The good news of the kingdom is not a message about something that happened in the past in the Holy Land, it is eternally in the present for Jesus loves us anew every day.

THE EIGHTH SUNDAY OF THE YEAR

First Reading: Hosea 2;16-17, 21-22

The prophet Hosea preached in the northern kingdom of Israel around 730BC, at a time when the people's prosperity had blinded them to the realisation that they would soon fall under the oppressive rule of the mighty Assyrian empire. Hosea appealed to the people to rediscover the covenant love of their God and he did so using the imagery of the love of a married couple. It appears that in his own life his wife had been unfaithful to him but he felt called by God to forgive her and to take her back.

Drawing on this experience, he compared God's love for Israel to that of a faithful husband who will never abandon his wife. The verses we read today are a description of the renewal of the covenant between Israel and God, not using the language of law but the language of love. The wilderness was the place where the chosen people first learned to put their trust in God and so this is the setting in which they can come to know the Lord once again.

Second Reading: 2 Corinthians 3:1-6
In all his writing, Paul frequently makes use of word-play to get his point across. He often uses contrasts between light and darkness or life and death to draw out the distinction between life with and without Jesus. In these verses, Paul is still persuading his readers of the validity of his mission and here he plays on the word 'letter'. He writes that the community in Corinth is a living letter of recommendation as to the value of his work. This is a letter not written with ink and not on tablets of stone (like the old Law) but rather written by the Spirit of God in their hearts. He wants them to recognise that the change that has occurred in their lives since coming to the knowledge of Christ is what matters and this shows that Paul was indeed God's instrument in bringing the good news to them.

Gospel: Mark 2:18-22
As the gospel of Mark continues, there is a growing sense of menace and opposition. Scribes had already objected to him forgiving sins and now people come to him to complain about the fact that other religious groups of the time seem to take their commitment more seriously by fasting, whereas Jesus' disciples do not. Jesus' answer is to focus on what is really taking place in him. He is not just another leader of a group expressing their religious fervour, he is in fact bringing in the new era of God's saving love, a time longed for by the Jews for centuries. He uses the biblical imagery of marriage and new wine to make his point. In the Old Testament God is likened to a bridegroom and wine is the symbol for joy and plenty in the psalms and prophetic writings. What is taking place in Jesus is not just a movement for reform, it is the fulfilment of the hopes of God's people for a better

world. A new way of thinking is called for when embracing the kingdom of God and its values.

Reflection

The two readings of today's Mass point to the fact that no matter what circumstances we find ourselves in it is always possible to see the hand of God at work, bringing good out of bad and healing where there has been hurt. Hosea's failed marriage would hardly have been considered as something which would lead to the writing of some of the most tender images for God in the scriptures, yet the prophet drew on his own experience of pain and heartbreak to express in a new way just how much Yahweh loves his people. So too Paul's struggles with the community in Corinth leads him to write about Christian ministry in a way that continues to encourage pastoral workers two thousand years later. In God, every situation, no matter how painful, is an opportunity for growth.

Ninth Sunday in Ordinary Time

First Reading: Deuteronomy 5:12-15

The Book of Deuteronomy is the last book of the Pentateuch and offers a summary of the review of God's covenant with Israel. It takes the form of the last will and testament of Moses just prior to his death and the entry of the chosen people into the Promised Land. Today's reading about the Sabbath is taken from the list of the 10 commandments. It should be noted that this list is also found with slight variations in the book of Exodus 20:2-17. One of the variations regards the reason for the Sabbath rest. In Exodus the people are to refrain from work just as God had rested on the seventh day and so it is a reminder to them that they share in the creative activity of God. In Deuteronomy, the reason given is that in honouring the day of rest they will recall the great act of liberation which brought them from slavery to freedom and so they will remember to treat their workers well. In both cases, the Sabbath commandment is a call to the awareness of the presence with them of their God who is both creator and saviour.

Second Reading 2 Corinthians 4:6-11

As we have already noted, some of Paul's critics in Corinth have questioned his authority as an apostle and have wondered how it is that his ministry has not been a glorious success. As ever, Paul's reply involves an appeal to the example of Christ's life and to the fact that God is working through weak human instruments to show how his power is truly at work in them. He willingly concedes that his ministry has met with obstacles and difficulties but this is not evidence of God's absence. On the contrary it shows how the true disciple shares in the passion of Jesus who never abandoned his mission but willingly went to the cross for the sake of us all. It also demonstrates that Paul is a profoundly hopeful person. He negotiates all the problems that life throws at him while firmly rooted in the hope that the gospel brings.

Gospel: Mark 2:23-3:6

This text contains two conflict stories that highlight the growing tension between Jesus and the religious authorities of his day. In both cases the dispute comes down to how one should read and interpret the Torah, the Law of Moses. The Pharisees were a lay group devoted to a scrupulous observance of the Law. They believed that such observance made them righteous, i.e. friends with God. Jesus, however, did not read the scriptures in this way at all. For him they are a witness to God's desire to save all people and any regulations they contain must be seen in this light. In the synagogue incident Jesus is depicted as being angry at the religious zeal of those who hold that obedience to the Law is more important that alleviating suffering. As far as Jesus is concerned their fervour is misplaced and offers a very distorted image of God. However, it is precisely these people who will conspire with others to put an end to Jesus' ministry. The Herodians referred to are supporters of King Herod and members of the political establishment in Galilee at the time. They are unlikely bedfellows of the Pharisees but their alliance indicates that the kingdom preached by Jesus threatened the religious and political world of his day.

Reflection

In our consumer-driven world, the notion of the Sabbath rest is widely neglected. This may, in part, be a response to an overly legalistic attitude from some quarters but it would be a great tragedy if we lost sight of the value of 'the Lord's day' as a special day in the week. The Bible shows us that we are called to this day of rest so that we can rediscover the truth about ourselves, namely that we have been created in the image and likeness of God and that as Christians we share in the power of the resurrection. These are reminders of our true dignity and destiny at a time when human beings are increasingly valued solely in terms of their economic worth.

THE TENTH SUNDAY IN ORDINARY TIME

First Reading: Genesis 3:9-15

These verses from the creation stories in Genesis are to be read not as a description of an historical event but as a narrative to explain how it is that in a good world created by God there is so much alienation and pain. This becomes clear in the verses following this text where God also addresses the woman and the man. In the ancient world there were many myths about human origins and the involvement of the gods. They often depicted the gods as completely arbitrary and unjust in their actions while human beings were mere pawns in their petty rows. In Genesis, however, the emphasis is on human dignity and freedom and how easily we can be tempted to reject the good. At the time of writing, the serpent was not identified with Satan; that approach came much later. In the early church the reference to the woman's offspring crushing the head of the serpent was interpreted as a prophecy concerning Jesus' victory over sin and death.

Second Reading: Corinthians 4:13-5:1

We continue our reading from Paul's defence of his ministry to the church in Corinth and he stays with the themes that he referred to earlier. Paul has no doubt that God called him and has sent him to the Corinthians so that they may hear the good news and enter into life in Christ. Therefore, even if he has to put up with all kinds of difficulties, they are as nothing compared to what awaits him, and indeed all believers. Our troubles in this life are transitory, but they play their part in preparing us for what lies ahead and help us to keep our focus on the things of God. There is a remarkable consistency in Paul's teaching and it always come back to what Christ has achieved through his passion, death and resurrection. In baptism we are incorporated into the mystery of Christ's dying and rising and it is this belief that gives Paul hope in the midst of his sufferings.

Gospel: Mark 3:20-35
There are four separate though connected incidents in this reading from Mark. The section begins and ends with reference to Jesus' family and in between we return to the conflict with the authorities. The question that links each part of the narrative is, 'What is the appropriate response to Jesus and his ministry?' The difficulty for his relatives at the beginning is that they fear he is losing his reason, perhaps because of the growing difficulties with the authorities. These tensions surface again as the Scribes assert that he is possessed. Jesus immediately rejects this charge and points out that his ministry is an attack on the forces of evil. He then goes further and charges them with a sin against the Holy Spirit for stating that what is clearly the work of God is in fact the work of the devil. This unforgivable sin is the willful refusal to recognise God's activity in what Jesus is doing. The section then reaches its climax with the arrival of Jesus' mother and brothers and they wish to speak with him. His answer to their request is to point out that the true relatives of Jesus are those who do the will of God. So the appropriate response to Jesus is to be with him in his doing of God's will. This forges a link that is greater than any blood relationship and highlights that inclusion in the kingdom is based on true conversion of heart and nothing else.

Reflection
In the first reading today it is noteworthy that God's first words to Adam after he had eaten the fruit were 'Where are you?' In a very succinct manner, that expresses what biblical revelation is all about: God searching for us and seeking to remove the barri-

ers that we constantly erect. Instead of rejoicing that we are made in God's image and likeness, we are forever making God in our image and likeness and thereby failing to grasp the infinite depth of his love. This is what is taking place with the scribes in today's narrative. However, when we seek to do God's will as embodied in the person of Jesus then we become part of his family and open ourselves up to the wonderful mystery of a truly gracious God.

THE ELEVENTH SUNDAY IN ORDINARY TIME

First Reading: Ezekiel 17:22-24

The prophet Ezekiel was a priest in the Temple in Jerusalem and was also one of the first wave of Judeans to be taken into exile in Babylonia in 597BC. He lived through this crisis and while still in exile heard of the destruction of the city and its temple in 587. This experience drove him to write much of what is in the book that bears his name today. There are two dominant themes: one is the sinfulness of the people that brought about such a disaster and the other is the faithfulness of God who will overturn this calamity. His language is highly symbolic and imaginative and had a considerable influence on the author of the Book of Revelation in the New Testament. Our short text for this Sunday was chosen because of its thematic link to the gospel but for the prophet his imagery of the great and fruitful tree that offers shade invites reflection on God's saving will. Yahweh alone is the one who can and will offer shade and protection to his people. They should not rely on the scheming of politicians and military alliances for their safety. Rather they should put their trust in God.

Second Reading: 2 Corinthians 5:6-10

The theme of hope mentioned last week is still to the fore as Paul continues with his reflection on his calling. There is a built-in tension between being able to continue with the Lord's work while being exiled from the Lord. He longs for the latter but knows the importance of the former and is prepared to bide his time until he is called to give an account of himself. He remains supremely confident that will be able to stand in the law courts of Christ to receive judgement for all that he did while still 'in the body'.

Gospel: Mark 4:26-34
While Mark places great emphasis on Jesus' role as a teacher and frequently uses this word to describe him, we are not given much detail about the content of his teaching. One exception to that is in chapter 4 where we hear a series of Jesus' parables of the kingdom. All the gospels agree that the parable was the primary means by which he taught the crowds and this was one of the main characteristics of his remarkable ministry. In this text there are two such parables about the kingdom, both centred on the theme of growth. In the first, the kingdom is likened to the situation that unfolds when someone sows seed in the ground. The seed grows independently of him, he knows not how, until the time of the harvest. Jesus wants his hearers to understand that as surely as the seed grows so too does the work of the kingdom happen. It is not up to us – it is a gift of God. The following parable says something similar, using language that echoes the words of Ezekiel from the first reading. The mustard seed is the tiniest of all but the shrub that issues from it is the greatest of all. So the kingdom, from insignificant beginnings, will grow to give shade to all who come to shelter in its branches.

Reflection
The unique message of Jesus is summed up by his use of the phrase 'kingdom of God' and his unique way of speaking about it was the parable. No doubt Jesus could have written a book or given a series of dogmas and rules, but he chose rather to tell short stories by way of illustration. The kingdom he speaks of is not the afterlife but an expression of how God wants the world to be. So the parables of the kingdom deal with God's will for the world and how his grace is at work around us. As such, they offer both comfort and challenge. Today's parables stress that we must not fret or worry but rather trust that the kingdom will come because God wants it to. They are an invitation to take time to consider how the plan of God unfolds around us in ways that are both surprising and sure.

THE TWELFTH SUNDAY IN ORDINARY TIME

First Reading: Job 38:1-11
The book of Job belongs to the wisdom tradition of the Old
Testament and is deservedly called a classic of world literature.
It deals with the problem of innocent suffering and the idea of a
just God, and does so through the eyes of Job, a good man who
experiences dreadful suffering though he has done nothing to
incur punishment. For most of the story Job argues his case with
his friends, who try to persuade him that since God is just his
suffering is somehow merited. Job stands his ground, refusing
to accept their explanation of his plight. Finally he demands that
God should take the stand and answer the charge that he is in
fact unjust. The reading for today marks the beginning of God's
reply, which consists of a series of unanswerable questions that
will force Job into conceding that proof of his innocence is not
evidence of God's guilt. The text is chosen because it portrays
God's sovereignty over the forces of nature, a point that is made
in today's gospel.

Second Reading: 2 Corinthians 5:14-17
Sometimes Paul's method of reasoning can be difficult to follow,
especially when he is presenting scriptural arguments to bolster
his case. There are other times, however, when his reasoning is
crystal clear and the power of his argument is overwhelming.
This reading is one such instance. He is using the words 'dead'
and 'alive' to highlight the effect of what Christ has achieved. He
died for us out of love so that we might be dead to ourselves and
alive to others. This is the remarkable mystery of the life of those
baptised into Christ. Paul makes the staggering claim that the
resurrection has changed everything and even those who knew
the earthly Jesus must now come to know him as the risen Christ
because what we have now is nothing less than a new creation, a
new world order.

Gospel: Mark 4:35-41
The dramatic story of the storm at sea brings into focus in a very
vivid manner the challenge of being in a relationship of faith
with Jesus. He has just finished teaching them about the king-

dom and its presence when he suggests that they cross to the other side. This is a dangerous suggestion for he is asking them, as it grows dark, to journey into the unknown, the pagan or Gentile side of the Sea of Galilee. Soon they find themselves in the midst of a storm with the waves swamping their small boat and their master asleep, apparently unconcerned. Their question to him says it all: 'Do you not care?' This plea gathers up the prayers of many who feel they are drowning in what can be a harsh and cruel world. Jesus hears their cry and, like God in the reading from Job, manifests his power by bringing calm into chaos. However, he also challenges them with a question that equals theirs for its relevance: 'Have you still no faith?' They have already seen him heal the sick, teach with authority and perform exorcisms, but something is missing as regards their attachment to him; a deep trust that indeed he does care.

Reflection
The storm at sea offers the perfect metaphor for expressing our doubts about faith. The power of nature can leave us feeling utterly insignificant; we are left powerless and totally at the mercy of the elements. So too life can appear incredibly difficult because of illness, bereavement, broken relationships and shattered dreams. At times, the image of sailing in a small boat, on a dark night, into the eye of a storm, perfectly describes how we are. At such times Jesus invites us to trust and it is only by doing it that we learn how.

THE THIRTEENTH SUNDAY IN ORDINARY TIME

First Reading: The Book of Wisdom 1:13-15, 2:23-24
This is probably the last book of the Old Testament to be written. It was addressed to well-educated, Greek-speaking Jews in Alexandria in Egypt and sought to show them how their faith could easily stand up to the logic of the philosophers who questioned its relevance. In the first five chapters the author addresses the problem of good and evil and stresses that we will be judged according to our deeds. In the verses of today's reading, he is making the point that death is not God's doing and for this teaching he is relying on the first chapters of Genesis. Death here

is not merely physical death but also spiritual death and this is not God's will for anyone. Rather we have been created for life and ultimately for eternal life with God. This is our destiny as human beings made in the image and likeness of God.

Second Reading: 2 Corinthians 8:7, 9, 11-15
The context for what Paul is saying here is the collection he organised for the Christian community in Jerusalem. He refers to it also in his first letter to the Corinthians (1 Cor 16:1-4) and we are told of it in Acts 24:17. In these verses Paul is using all his persuasive powers to encourage his hearers to be generous in their giving. Firstly he praises them for the abundance of gifts and talents they have and the fact that they are held in such high esteem by Paul himself. He then points to the example of Jesus himself who displayed the greatest generosity by forsaking everything that was his for their sake. However, Paul also makes it clear that he does not want them to be in hardship themselves over this collection. They have to strike a balance between their surplus and the needs of their brethren in Jerusalem. For Paul, this collection was not only a matter of charity but was to be symbolic of the unity in love that should exist between Gentile and Jewish Christians.

Gospel: Mark 5:21-43
There are two miracle stories in this quite long extract from Mark and they demonstrate an important theme and character-istic of this gospel. The first thing we notice is that the story of the raising of the daughter of Jairus begins the sequence, but then is cut off as we consider the woman with the haemorrhage. It is sometimes referred to as a sandwich technique and it is a characteristic of Mark, used to hold our interest as he develops an idea by means of two different stories. It quickly becomes ap-parent that the overarching theme is the need for faith. In the story of the woman, her willingness to trust in Jesus is total but by contrast the people in the house of Jairus laugh at him when he suggests the child is only asleep. Jesus tells the woman who touched him that her faith made her well, and to the people an-nouncing the news of the death of the little girl he says: 'Do not be afraid, only have faith.' We have only already learned

through the preaching of Jesus and his parables that the kingdom is present in his ministry and that it is both a gift and a challenge. Living by faith is the challenge but it is also the way to healing and new life for those who embrace the message with trust and confidence.

Reflection
At first glance, there may not seem to be much connection between these readings but an incident from the life of Gerard Manley Hopkins might shed some light on the strong link that is there. Someone once wrote to the poet asking how he could come to know God. Hopkins wrote back with the simple answer: 'Give alms.' The God who wills us to live eternally cannot be known in theory or theology – he can only be truly known through love. That is our calling as Christians. If we understand that we have been made rich through the poverty of Jesus then we cannot but reach out to others.

THE FOURTEENTH SUNDAY IN ORDINARY TIME

First Reading: Ezekiel 2:2-5
The prophet Ezekiel lived during the worst crisis endured by the Israelites in the Old Testament. He was a priest in the Jerusalem Temple at the time when the Babylonian armies invaded Judea, besieged the city and finally destroyed it and its holiest shrine. His mission, like that of his contemporary Jeremiah, was to point out to the people the inevitability of the calamity that was to befall them and this is what is spoken about in this reading. God calls the prophet to speak to the people even though it is clear that they will pay him no heed. However, because of the power of his word and the strength of his character they will indeed know that a prophet is speaking to them. The rest of the Book of Ezekiel outlines the content of his preaching and the strange visions through which he discerned the message of God. Although he roundly condemns the Israelites for their infidelity, he holds out a message of hope for a new and bright future made possible through the faithfulness of God.

Second Reading: 2 Corinthians 12:7-10

In the last part of this letter, Paul finds himself once again in the position of having to defend himself against his detractors. His defence begins in chapter 10 and by the time we reach this part he has explained all that he has been through for the sake of the gospel. He has endured many hardships but he has also been blessed by God with mystical experiences. Just in case, however, that he become proud he now informs them of an experience of suffering which brought him very low. It is not known exactly what he is referring to when he speaks of this 'thorn in the flesh' but what is clear is that it caused him great distress. His repeated prayers to be freed from this affliction were met with an answer that taught him that God was at work through it all, teaching him to depend not on himself but rather on God's strength working through his weakness.

Gospel: Mark 6:1-6

This incident reports what happened when Jesus returned home to Nazareth for the first time after beginning his public ministry and having much success all around Galilee. It continues to deal with the topic of faith and obstacles to it. As in Luke's account, the beginning is quite promising. Jesus amazes them by his teaching in the synagogue but their amazement quickly turns to resistance as their supposed knowledge of him convinces them that he could not possibly be anyone special. The reference to his brothers is usually understood in the Catholic tradition as meaning his kin or cousins. In Greek Orthodox circles, there is a tradition that Joseph had children by an earlier marriage and these are Jesus' stepbrothers. The lack of faith that Jesus encounters leads the evangelist to comment that he could do no miracle there and that he was amazed at their lack of faith.

Reflection

Ezekiel and Paul both provide us with a valuable lesson in discipleship in these readings. Their work for God brings them into situations that they would not choose for themselves and appears on occasions to meet with failure. However, they have both learned that if they keep their focus on the Lord of the work then they need have no worries about their work for the Lord.

All their experiences can be of service to him if undergone in a spirit of humble faith. Similarly, it is the lack of just such a humble faith that prohibits the spread of the kingdom in Nazareth.

THE FIFTEENTH SUNDAY IN ORDINARY TIME

First Reading: Amos 7:12-15
The prophet Amos is the earliest of the so-called writing prophets, that is those prophets who have a book named after them. He lived in the eighth century BC, at a time when the people of Israel were divided into two kingdoms. One was in the north with its capital in Samaria, the other was in Judea and its capital was Jerusalem. At the time of Amos, the Northern Kingdom was enjoying considerable prosperity but it was at the expense of the poor and vulnerable and this was in direct contravention of the covenant with Yahweh. Although Amos was from the south and a farmer with no obvious religious background, he felt called by God to go Bethel which was the shrine of the Northern Kingdom. There he proclaimed a series of dire warnings against the ruling and wealthy classes for their oppression of the poor. Such a message was not well received and in the reading for today we see how the high priest of the shrine demands that Amos go back home and mind his own business. Amos' reply is simple and direct: 'I am only doing what God sent me to do.'

Second Reading: Ephesians 1:3-14
These verses, from the opening chapter of the letter, replace Paul's usual words of thanksgiving addressed to the local community with a long prayer of praise and blessing to God. In essence, Paul is summarising the meaning of the life, death and resurrection of Christ and celebrating the fact that this is a pouring forth of the grace of God in a way never before imagined. Jews and Gentiles now share fully in the plan of God to bring all peoples to holiness. This intention of God was a mystery which only in the present age has been revealed through Jesus. It means that the divisions between peoples have now been broken down because we have all been granted forgiveness and so are truly free. The active presence of the Holy Spirit among those who believe is the guarantee of what has taken place.

Gospel: Mark 6:7-13

After his apparent lack of success in Nazareth, Jesus embarks on the next stage of the work of spreading the kingdom. He challenges his apostles to share in his radical trust in the Father as they go forward, believing that the power they have is from God and knowing that the message is one of repentance – that is, true conversion of heart. Their task is an urgent one and they are not to delay. It is worth recalling that when they were first called by Jesus it was 'to be with him'. Now, having been with him and coming to know him, they are empowered to do as he has done.

Reflection

These readings show us two sides of the same coin that is faith in God. A genuine faith involves both a grateful recognition of what is given and also a desire to be changed from within and to live accordingly. The people Amos was talking to had plenty of religion – they said their prayers on the Sabbath and offered sacrifices to their God – but this was merely ritual and they had no compunction in exploiting their fellow citizens for the rest of the week. On the other hand, in his writing to the Ephesians Paul is completely overwhelmed by the realisation of what God has done for us for in Christ and he cannot but pour out his thanks and praise. When it comes to being disciples, Jesus asks us to develop a habit of trust. This is not a blind faith but a willingness to really come to know him and be changed from within. It is only then that we can share in his mission.

THE SIXTEENTH SUNDAY IN ORDINARY TIME

First Reading: Jeremiah 23:1-6

Time and again the prophets of the Old Testament condemned the failure of the leaders of the chosen people to lead them in the ways of God. The most frequently used image when talking about authentic leadership was that of the shepherd, for just as God was the Shepherd of Israel so the leaders ought to mirror Yahweh's care for his people. In this reading, Jeremiah rounds on those responsible for the impending tragedy of the destruction of Jerusalem and the exile to Babylon of those who survive. However, he also offers a word of hope, saying that in the future

God will bring those exiles back home and raise up shepherds for the people who will indeed be true to their task. This means that there need never again be fear and terror in the lives of God's chosen ones. God will send them a virtuous king, a descendent of David to rule with integrity. This prophecy is depicted as fulfilled in today's gospel but not in the throne room of a Jerusalem palace but rather in the desolate places where the hungry are to be found.

Second Reading: Ephesians 2:13-18
This remarkable reading offers us the basis for understanding the importance of reconciliation as both a gift of God and also a task for the church. Paul argues that by his death on the cross Jesus has broken down the dividing wall that used to exist between Jews and pagans. This is because now all peoples are recognised as children of God. It is no longer a matter of observing the Law of Moses but of each person coming to God through the work of the Spirit. Christ is the New Man who is creating a new humanity, united around him and living in peace. Since it is God who has reconciled us, how then can we persist with our hostilities?

Gospel: Mark 6:30-34
This text follows on from what happened last Sunday when Jesus missioned them as his apostles. If their success depends on their being sent by Jesus, then to some extent it also depends on their returning to him. In other words, it only makes sense because of their relationship to him and this is what is demonstrated in this short text. They return to him, no doubt full of all that had happened to them but also tired and so he suggests time apart. Such is the hunger for the good news of the kingdom that they don't even have time to eat. However, the people know the lake shore and can guess where they are headed for and so, on arrival, Jesus and the apostles are greeted by a large crowd. Jesus' response, however, is not one of frustration but of compassion and the apostles learn once again from the Master what it means to be a shepherd. It is also noteworthy that what Jesus does for this large crowd is not to perform miracles but to teach them at length, thus highlighting again that vital aspect of Jesus' ministry.

Reflection

It is a sad reflection on two thousand years of Christianity that there are still so many divisions among those who claim to follow Christ. However, this is a reminder to us that reconciliation is not something that we merely wish for or give approval to. Being reconciled to those from whom we are estranged can be very difficult. Wounds do not easily heal and recognising our need to forgive and be forgiven takes courage and humility. The readings remind us that our faith response to the difficulties we face as a church must always be rooted in the compassion of God. We are also reminded that teaching and learning will always be part of what we do as a Christian community.

THE SEVENTEENTH SUNDAY IN ORDINARY TIME

First Reading: 2 King 4:42-44

The Prophet Elisha took over from Elijah as the one who witnessed to God's presence with the people in times of crisis. Today's story takes place during a time of famine and is one of a series of stories which illustrate the power of the prophet. It has obvious echoes with the gospel for today, which is the story of the multiplication of the loaves and fishes. It is important to remember that many of the miracles of Jesus have parallels in the Old Testament, for this shows that the compassion of God is something known and celebrated long before the time of Jesus. Yahweh's desire to save his people, frequently expressed through the image of food, comes to its fullest expression in Jesus the Bread of Life. Elisha's concern in this story is not just for himself but for the poor who are with him. The food is brought to him but he readily shares it and so there is enough for all.

Second Reading: Ephesians 4:1-6

In moving towards the conclusion of the letter, Paul now begins to advise the communities on how to live out their faith in Christ. In keeping with the themes of unity and reconciliation that we have already seen in the letter, Paul reminds them of the need for a selfless concern for those around them. Unity is important because it gives a powerful witness to the presence of God with them and this unity is maintained and strengthened when they practise the virtues of patience and gentleness. The context for the letter is Paul's imprisonment and indeed may be shortly before his martyrdom, so that gives added weight to his appeal that they should recognise that they all have one Father.

Gospel: John 6:1-15

For the next five Sundays we set aside our reading of the gospel of Mark to devote attention to John 6 and the Bread of Life discourse. The fourth gospel differs from the others in many respects and one is the way in which the evangelist teases out the implications of Jesus' actions through long discussions in which the participants are being asked to consider in depth the symbolism behind his deeds. The multiplication of the loaves and fishes is the only miracle story that John shares with the other gospels, though he calls them signs because of his desire to highlight not so much the power of Jesus but his *identity*. The signs point to who he is as the one sent by the Father. John's account of this differs in some small ways. He tells us these events take place just before the feast of Passover and thereby invites us to make a connection with that founding story of the Israelites when God fed them in the wilderness. He also notes that the boy brings five 'barley loaves' which was the bread of the poor. Finally, we are told that twelve baskets of scraps are gathered up so that nothing may be lost. Here it is possible to see a symbolism referring to Jesus' desire to gather to himself the new people of God.

Reflection

It is not given to us to perform miracles like Elisha and Jesus but perhaps that is as it should be. In a world where there is so much need, we have a great deal to give. It may not seem like much to us but when it is shared it becomes more than we can ever imagine. The miracles worked by Jesus and Elisha needed someone to come along and offer what they had. God still needs us to do the same and still guarantees that if we do, things will happen! That we are reading from John over the next few weeks is an invitation to realise that while all the gospels proclaim Jesus, they do so differently. This means that we need to read them differently so that we can get the most from what the evangelist is trying to say. Very early on in the tradition of the church, John's was called the 'spiritual gospel' because from the beginning it was recognised that he was challenging us to think very deeply about the mystery of the Word made flesh.

THE EIGHTEENTH SUNDAY IN ORDINARY TIME

First Reading: Exodus 16:2-4, 12-15
These verses from Exodus come shortly after the account of the parting of the sea by Yahweh and the escape of the Israelites from the armies of the Pharaoh. Now, however, they complain that Moses has brought them out into the wilderness to starve them to death. The fickle and self-serving aspect of our human nature is very much to the fore in the story. Nonetheless, God hears their complaint and promises to send them food. This manna, bread from heaven, will nourish them and be a reminder to them during their desert wanderings that God is indeed with them. Efforts to explain the phenomenon by recourse to science and certain natural occurrences in the desert miss the point of the narrative, which is a challenge to the chosen people to put their trust in the God who saves them and is faithful no matter what.

Second Reading: Ephesians 4:17, 24-35
Paul continues with this final exhortation when he advises the community on how they must put into practice what they have learned since becoming disciples of Christ. If they are converts from paganism (rather than Judasim) then this new faith they have embraced stands in sharp contrast to the religions of the Greco-Roman world. These were characterised by superstitious beliefs and practices and a sense that one's fate was predetermined. Only by the use of magic or mystery religions could people hope to escape their destiny. What they heard about Christ was a rejection of all that and offered them instead the love of a personal God, whose Spirit living within them was a source of transforming power.

Gospel: John 6:24-35

We return here to the fallout from Jesus' miracle of the loaves and fishes. The crowd is depicted as searching enthusiastically for Jesus but when they find him he confronts them on their motivation, saying they must look beyond their full stomachs to see what God is saying to them through what has taken place. What God is asking of them is that they believe in the one he has sent. In the fourth gospel faith is not a concept, it is an activity. Believing in Jesus is the equivalent of doing the work that God wants because it involves a personal relationship, an abiding in him. However, the crowd don't understand and look for a sign such as their ancestors received. The irony is that they have just such a sign in front of them but they fail to see it. Jesus tells them he is the true bread, not like the manna, but the bread of God's word that satisfies the deepest human hunger. They are invited to nourish themselves on the bread of life, in other words to come to know and believe in Jesus. At this point in the narrative the evangelist is not yet speaking about the Eucharist – that will come later. Here he is making use of the Old Testament symbolism of wisdom as nourishment to speak of Jesus as the only one who can satisfy our hunger for God.

Reflection

We only have to consider the number of cookery programmes on television to realise that food is big business and that it has little to do with feeding the hungry. In the developed world it is about novelty, the exotic, what is really healthy. We don't want the same old thing over and over because we get bored easily. In a certain sense, this type of hunger is a potent symbol for what is being spoken about in the readings. To quote from Deuteronomy, 'Human beings do not live on bread alone but on every word that comes from the mouth of God.' We hunger for meaning, a sense of purpose and if that is addressed then we can be truly content. This is what Jesus, as the bread of life, is speaking about. In him we can come to understand ourselves and be amazed at our own dignity and worth in the sight of God. We are, at heart, spiritual beings and if we don't address that, then we might easily spend our time satisfying our appetites and never our deepest need.

The Nineteenth Sunday in Ordinary Time

First Reading: 1 Kings 19:4-8

This short reading is taken from a story which tells of the Prophet Elijah's flight from Israel in an effort to escape the anger of King Ahab and his wife Jezebel who he has condemned for their idolatry. He is feeling that his ministry has been a disaster and wishes that he were dead. However, he is quickly roused from this state of sorrow and depression and told to eat what has been put before him because he will need the nourishment for what lies ahead. Having taken the food, he sets out on his journey to the mountain of God, Sinai, the place where Moses and the children of Israel encountered God and received the law. In the verses following these we are told that once there, he too finds God, not in a glorious manifestation like that experienced by his ancestors but in the quiet breeze that calls to him. He is renewed in his vocation and, returning to Israel, he continues his prophetic mission.

Second Reading: Ephesians 4:30-5:2

We are now in the final section of the letter that consists of a series of appeals to the communities to conduct their lives in accordance with the message they have received. Earlier in the letter they have been told how the church is the body of Christ and that the walls of division between Jews and Gentiles have been broken down. Since they are one united people in Christ, sealed by the Holy Spirit, they must not make the Spirit sad by behaviour which is contrary to the gospel. The love and forgiveness that characterised the life of Christ must be the hallmark of their lives too.

Gospel: 6:41-51

One of the techniques used frequently in the gospel of John is that of misunderstanding. In the case of Nicodmeus and the Samaritan woman they misunderstand his words about being born again (3:4) and living water (4:15) and this leads to further revelation or explanation by Jesus. Now those who hear Jesus saying that he is the bread of life come down from heaven fail to grasp the significance of the statement and insist that they know where he is from. Jesus, however, continues with his revelatory discourse and shows how he is indeed the one sent by God to give life. To believe in Jesus is come to life, a life that never ends. We come to this life through believing in Jesus who offers his life (flesh) for the sake of the world. Until now, in using the symbol of bread the focus has been on believing in who Jesus is, but with the change in language from bread to flesh there will be a shift in meaning towards a reflection on his death on the cross and the Eucharist. The gospel of John does not make for easy reading because of its layers of meaning and great depth but it offers great inspiration if we but try.

Reflection
We are invited to recognise ourselves in the Elijah story as people who, if they are to be faithful on the journey, need to be sustained. We can easily become dispirited either at our own shortcomings or at the failings of others. However, as we are often reminded in the scriptures, we must learn to rely not only on our own resources but on the guiding presence of God that directs our life. It is probably true to say that it is almost a necessity in our journey of faith that we come to a low point. In the biblical tradition and in that of the church, all the heroes and heroines come to a stage where they too have to acknowledge their own weakness and utter dependence on God. This does not come easily to us because it can seem like failure. That is when we need to remind ourselves of what the Lord said to Paul: 'My grace is sufficient for you, for power is made perfect in weakness.' (2 Cor 12:9)

THE TWENTIETH SUNDAY IN ORDINARY TIME

First Reading: Proverbs 9:1-6
The Book of Proverbs, which is found among the wisdom writings of the Old Testament, is made up of a collection of wise sayings along with some reflections on the nature of wisdom and the importance of seeking it. The first section of the book deals explicitly with the value of wisdom and it is from the end of this section that our reading is taken. In this extract, wisdom is presented as a woman who has prepared a banquet of the finest food and who is now inviting everyone to come and be nour-

ished at her table. In chapter 1, wisdom was also described as a woman who goes through the streets seeking disciples who will pay heed to her words. This personification of wisdom would later play a very important role in helping the writers of the New Testament to explain Jesus' identity as the wisdom of God. In the gospel for today, Jesus describes himself as the living bread which has come down from heaven. He is the one who shows us that the word of God is the bread we need to be truly alive.

Second Reading: Ephesians 5:5-15

The advice to the Christians of Ephesus continues in this short reading which once again lays a particular stress on the role of the Holy Spirit. The point is made here by a series of contrasts in which they are urged to behave like intelligent and not foolish people. The world in which they live may be wicked but their lives should be pointing the way to another reality and so, by living according to the gospel, they are helping to redeem the world. They are told to give time to recognising what is the will of the Lord and not to be thoughtless. The result of such a lifestyle is that they will learn to sing the praises of God in all the circumstances of their lives, giving thanks to him through the power of the Spirit who lives in them.

Gospel: John 6:51-58

We begin here, where we left off last week, with further misunderstanding of Jesus by the crowds. Clearly Jesus is not speaking of cannibalism and so he takes the image further by talking of his flesh and blood. Partaking in his flesh and blood means believing in him and in his life-giving death. Through their faith they are in communion with him and that communion is expressed through the Eucharist. The believer comes to live in him and draws life from him just as Jesus himself drew life from the Father. Everything here must be viewed from the perspective of Jesus' death on the cross. Through the Eucharist we come to live by the same self sacrificing love that brought Jesus to Calvary. It is striking that in John's account of the last supper there is no reference to Eucharist but rather a depiction of Jesus washing the disciples' feet. John shows us the Eucharist in action and this is a reminder that the union with Jesus offered through Holy Communion cannot be thought of in some purely personal, devotional way. Jesus gives himself to us so that we can give ourselves to others.

Reflection
Even though the first reading today may be two and an half thousand years old, the call to seek wisdom and reject foolishness has a very contemporary ring to it. Human nature does not change but we are slow to learn from experience. Today, life itself on this wonderful planet is threatened by our folly and a refusal to recognise that our actions have consequences. Instead of feasting ourselves at the sustainable banquet at Wisdom's house, we prefer to go blindly on gorging ourselves and ignoring the fact that God has called us to a responsible stewardship of his creation. Our celebration of the Eucharist should be a weekly reminder to us that we are all called to a life-giving relationship with God, with one another and with the planet we share.

THE TWENTY-FIRST WEEK IN ORDINARY TIME

First Reading: Joshua 24:1-2, 15-18
The Book of Joshua tells the story of how the Israelites were guided by God in their conquest of the land of Canaan. Having crossed the wilderness for forty years they finally reached the Promised Land but they were then faced with the task of subduing the peoples who inhabited the land. They faced overwhelming odds but because God was with them they triumphed and our reading for today describes the situation at the end of the book. Having taken possession of Canaan, Joshua assembles all the tribes of Israel at Shechem in order to have a covenant renewal ceremony. This was to be an opportunity for them to rededicate themselves to the covenant they had made with Yahweh at Mount Sinai. Joshua puts the case to them very simply: 'Choose today whom you wish to serve.' The people give a resounding 'yes' to the Lord and pledge themselves to continue serving him and not to be like the nations around them. Throughout the Old Testament story of the people of God there is a recurring theme of the need for each generation to decide

once again whether they wish to continue the special relationship, based on justice and love, which the covenant offers them.

Second Reading: Ephesians 5:21-32
The exhortation to continue living in a way which is consistent with the gospel continues in our reading from Ephesians. In this section Paul addresses himself to married couples and seeks to draw out for them the implications for their relationship of being Christian. To appreciate what he is saying we must remember that in the Greco-Roman society in which Paul lived, the lines of authority and subservience were clearly drawn. Husbands, parents and masters all had power and control over their wives, children and slaves. In addressing this situation Paul does not propose a radical abolition of the existing order; rather he says that all relationships must be lived out in the light of Christ's love. It is the relationship with Jesus which determines all the others and this calls for change. Paul, as a man of his time, does not question that the husband is the head of the house but he proposes that the manner of his leadership must be like that of Christ, one of service and self giving. It is unfortunate that his teaching is sometimes used to support male dominance in marriage when what he is calling for is a relationship in which the couple 'give way to one another in Christ'.

Gospel: John 6:60-69
We come now to the last extract from John's gospel and the end of the discourse on the Bread of Life. It highlights a theme that began in chapter 5 of John and that is a growing opposition to and refusal to believe in Jesus. While earlier in the discourse it was the crowds who were having difficulty with Jesus' presentation of himself as the bread of life, now it is his own disciples who are complaining that it is too much to expect them to accept what Jesus has said about himself. Jesus replies that what he is speaking about can only be understood through the work of the spirit, i.e. through the eyes of faith. Some find the challenge too much and cease to follow him and in response Jesus asks the twelve do they also wish to go away. Peter replies with a confession of faith that demonstrates that he (and they!) are beginning to grasp something of the revelation that Jesus brings. Because

they believe then they know that he is indeed the Holy One of God.

Reflection

'What about you, do you also want to go away?' No-one can be press-ganged into discipleship and Jesus yet again puts the choice before us as we gather for our Sunday Eucharist. Why is there a crisis here? Is it because they cannot believe that Jesus can truly give of himself in the way he has described? Is faith in the Eucharist too much to ask for? Perhaps it is not so much an intellectual difficulty about how this can happen but rather an intuition about the far reaching implications of what he is saying. For in giving us himself he is asking us to forget about ourselves and maybe that is just too much. Yet Peter speaks for us all when he says: 'Lord to whom shall we go?' Nothing in the world with all its possibilities and attractions can nourish our hunger to love and be loved as completely as Jesus, our Bread of Life.

THE TWENTY-SECOND SUNDAY IN ORDINARY TIME

First Reading: Deuteronomy 4:1-2, 6-8

This reading sums up very well the themes of the Book of Deuteronomy which was probably written hundreds of years after the events it describes. It is presented as the last will and testament of Moses given to the people before they cross over into the Promised Land. Moses is reminding them of all that God has done for them and how they are now bound to him by the covenant and its commandments. The entire book is an appeal to remain faithful, recognising that God has gifted them not only with the land but also with true wisdom and it is this which sets them apart from the other nations. A word that occurs many times in Deuteronomy and twice in this reading is 'today' and this shows how God's saving acts are not to be considered as events in the remote past but ongoing manifestations of his love.

Second Reading: James 1:17-18, 21-22, 27

This letter was not addressed to any one community but to the church in general and so it is known as one of the 'catholic' epis-

tles (the original meaning of catholic being universal). The issues it addresses are therefore not the particular problems of
any one group but reflect the demands which Christian living
makes on all peoples at all times. Since James was a Jew he
writes with a passion for justice like that which is found in the
prophets and in the wisdom writings of the Old Testament.

This reading opens with the recognition of God's goodness
in gifting the church with the message of the good news. This
message is not a static commandment to be obeyed but a seed
which, once planted, has to be nourished. This will only happen
if we truly listen to the word of God and act upon it. Such an understanding of faith leads on to a very important definition of
religion which stresses, on the one hand, its' practical and social
dimension while, on the other, the need not to become swal-
lowed up by worldly concerns.

Gospel: Mark 7:1-8, 14-15, 21-23
As we return to Mark we find ourselves in yet another story of
conflict between Jesus and his opponents. Here the Pharisees are
reprimanding the followers of Jesus for not engaging in ritual
washing before they eat. This is an example of a tradition handed
down in Pharisee circles which had come to have the full force of
the written Law. Jesus has little time for their legalism and
quotes from Isaiah to make his point. This is only lip service to
God who does not care about their external observances but
who desires a true worship of the heart. A person cannot be
made unclean by external factors, eg the failure to observe purely
religious ritual; rather we are made unclean by that which
comes from within, from our hearts, the source of our moral action.

Reflection
If a survey were to be conducted among churchgoers in which
they were asked for a definition of religion it is unlikely that
many would come up with the simple answer provided by
James. Coming to the help of orphans and widows would be for
many a kind of agreeable by-product of religion whereas James
places it right at the centre of who we are and what we do. This
is surely a message for today when so many people go to such

great lengths in their search for wisdom and the knowledge of God. A religion that can be observed at a purely external level has a certain appeal. It is easy to feel we are making progress and that we are better than those who do not measure up. We imagine that by our own efforts we can come close to God. However, Jesus wants no part in such a sham. He is concerned with the heart and a faith that does justice.

THE TWENTY-THIRD SUNDAY IN ORDINARY TIME

First Reading: Isaiah 35:4-7
We cannot be sure of the exact historical circumstances in which these wonderful, inspirational words of the prophet were written. During the prophet's own lifetime there were many occasions when his people were close to despair. However, Isaiah had an unshakable faith in the trustworthiness of God and it was such a faith that allowed him to see a future in which God's will for the world would come to fruition. It is such a vision that is offered to us in this reading. The words 'vengeance' and 'retribution' may have a negative overtone and might suggest a punishing or judgemental God. Isaiah, however, uses them to show God as the kinsman who is coming to the defence of his family. God is like one who is obliged to come to the aid of his kinsfolk when they are crushed and oppressed. So the action of God in this reading is transforming. People who have been trapped by their infirmities can now shout out with joy as they see their desert turned into a fertile place of growth and new life. In the gospels the evangelists pointed to the ministry of Jesus as the time when this prophecy was fulfilled.

Second Reading: James 2:1-5
The clear and simple definition of religion which was offered last week is now followed by very down-to-earth advice as to how all Christian communities should conduct themselves. The good news means that God shows no partiality and that we are all equally his children. So it would be an outrage for the community to show favour to individuals on account of their wealth or social standing and James drives the point home with an example which is as relevant today as when it was first written.

Making a fuss over a wealthy benefactor at the liturgy while at the same time humiliating a poor person makes nonsense of what we say we believe. Unfortunately, as church history has shown time and again, we can all too easily fall into the trap James is speaking about.

Gospel: Mark 7:31-37

This week stories of conflict are left behind as we are treated to further evidence of what Jesus' ministry of proclaiming the kingdom of God is all about. The story begins with a rather flawed geography lesson. The sequence mentioned by Mark makes no sense but it may be that he is making a theological point because the places he mentions are the gentile surroundings of Galilee where the kingdom has been first proclaimed. The man brought to Jesus cannot hear or speak and is therefore cut off from the good news, but through Jesus' healing touch he is restored and the response to this action is one of unrestrained praise and wonder. The people realise that in Jesus all that the prophets had spoken of so long ago is being fulfilled and Mark is also making the point that this ministry embraces Jew and Gentile alike.

Reflection

By the time of Jesus many religious traditions were in place which served to differentiate between those who were on the inside and those who were outsiders. This led to divisions, inequality and oppression – the very things that the covenant was supposed to eradicate. So when Jesus reached out to the poor, to sinners and those on the margins he was bringing into focus once again the kind of world God wanted. His was a love that included everyone and which could not be bought. In commanding that the ears of the deaf man be opened there is a message to us all, especially those who think that their hearing is perfect. Our ability to really hear the good news can be limited by many things, especially closed minds and hearts. Perhaps as individuals and as a community our prayer during this Sunday Eucharist might be that we would be opened to all the transformation that God wants to work in us.

TWENTY FOURTH SUNDAY IN ORDINARY TIME

First Reading: Isaiah 50:5-9
In the middle section of the Book of the Prophet Isaiah there are four striking poems which have become known as the Songs of the Servant. Today's reading is the third of these poems and like the others deals with the relationship between Yahweh and this unnamed person who is simply called the servant. This person is reflecting on an experience of suffering and rejection and showing how even in the most adverse circumstances he had come to understand that God was with him. We are not told exactly what had taken place but the language suggests that false accusations were being made against him. The suffering servant remains strong in the face of abuse and insults because he firmly believes that God will vindicate him. The Servant's Songs were later to become very important in the early church where they were understood as prophecies of Jesus' passion and death.

Second Reading: James 2:14-18
We have already seen how James has stressed the importance of a practical religion which seeks to help out those in need. In this reading he develops the idea into showing the necessary connection between faith and works. Experience teaches us that religion can easily become very inward looking, concentrating only on one's personal relationship with God to the exclusion of everything else. Such religious people may say many prayers and be very devoted to the things of God, but if this piety blinds them to the material needs of those around them then it is quite useless. In fact James goes so far as to say it is dead. Once again he is showing a link with the great prophets of the Old Testament who insisted that all the burnt offerings in the Jerusalem Temple were worthless if the people sacrificing there turned their back on the plight of the poor.

Gospel: Mark 8:27-35
We come now to a crucial moment in Mark's narrative as we hear the first of three predictions of Jesus' passion and death. From the beginning of the gospel there have been many expressions of wonder and amazement at what Jesus has done and

these have often been accompanied by the question: 'Who can this be?' Jesus, however, has attempted to keep a lid on the question of his identity, as though he wanted it kept a secret. Now in these important verses we learn why. Jesus is interested above all in the response of faith and that is why he asks the disciples: 'Who do you say that I am?' Peter answers, acknowledging that Jesus is the Messiah. This is a Hebrew word and simply means the anointed one, but in the minds of the Jews of first-century Palestine it means much more. Peter is saying that Jesus is the long awaited fulfilment of the scriptures, the one to set his people free from foreign domination and who would usher in a great period of restoration and renewal. Jesus accepts the title but immediately begins the task of trying to bring his disciples to understand that he is not the type of Messiah they expect. Quite the opposite in fact, for the kingdom he proclaims will meet with fierce opposition and he will suffer the ultimate penalty for his faithfulness to it. What's more is that he expects his disciples to walk the same path.

Reflection

As Christians we pray daily using the words Jesus taught us: 'Thy Kingdom come.' When we do this we are saying that we want the world to be the way God wants it. In other words a place of peace and justice where no-one suffers through poverty, war or oppression. If this is what we want then we must live in a way which helps to bring this about, we must be committed to change. Such a choice might leave us like the Servant in the first reading facing abuse and insults from those who would prefer to leave things as they are. This is what Jesus is talking about in today's gospel: taking up our cross to follow him does not mean we are to go looking for suffering; rather it means accepting that choosing the way of God's kingdom will cost us. In short, faith without works is dead!

THE TWENTY-FIFTH SUNDAY IN ORDINARY TIME

First Reading: Wisdom 2:12, 17-20
The Book of Wisdom is the latest of the Old Testament books
and may have been written only some 60 years before the birth
of Jesus. It probably originated in Alexandria and was intended
for Greek-speaking Jews who lived in that great city and who
were constantly under pressure to abandon their faith for the
ways of the surrounding Greco-Roman culture. The author reminds them of their Jewish traditions and, like the other late
books of the Old Testament, it stresses how each person must
stand before God for judgement. Therefore, they must not lose
heart when they are persecuted for their faith as they surely will
be. To live a life of virtue is to be a child of God and such a life is
an unwelcome challenge to those who live only for themselves.
These are the 'godless' ones mentioned at the beginning of the
reading who are seeking to do away with the just person.

Second Reading: James 3:16-4:3
It will be clear by now that the letter of James is characterised by
a clear and direct style which quickly gets to the heart of the
matter. There is further evidence of this in today's reading when
the author addresses the problem of divisions and rivalries in
the community. He points out that such problems are the result
of jealousy and ambition and he contrasts this with the wisdom
that is from above. Its presence makes for peace and harmony
and is only concerned with doing good. It ensures that there will
be neither partiality nor hypocrisy, both of which have already
been condemned in the letter. The next question must be: how
then can we attain this wisdom and overcome our ambitions
and rivalries? For James the answer lies in prayer and a kind of
prayer which seeks the good of the other above all else. Such
prayer takes us out of ourselves and leads us on the path to wisdom.

Gospel: Mark 9:30-37
Following from last Sunday and the first passion prediction we
come now to the second time in Mark when Jesus speaks about
what awaits him in Jerusalem. However, the reader of the

gospel is invited to see in these not some knid of proof that Jesus can tell the future but rather an attempt by Jesus to persuade his disciples that they need to change their attitude towards him and his ministry. It is clear that the disciples are happy to be with Jesus as their long awaited and triumphant Messiah but they are failing completely in that Jesus is not interested such discipleship. He wants them to learn the way of the kingdom which is the way of the cross. This is not the path to glory as human beings understand it but to humble service and love. In taking the child as an example, he is saying to his followers, 'Be concerned for those who can offer you nothing in return, the powerless and the vulnerable. When you welcome them you welcome the true Messiah and the God who sent him.'

Reflection
Today's readings are dealing with wisdom but from different perspectives. In the first, people who are caught up in them-selves want to be rid of the wise person because his life points up the emptiness of their own. In the second, we see the conse-quences of choosing to live by the wisdom of God. The wise per-son is not necessarily rich, popular or successful and while these maybe the values which are esteemed in our modern culture they do not compare with being at peace with ourselves. This is the fruit of wisdom and is a gift to be prayed for with all our hearts. In the gospel, Jesus offers us the wisdom of the cross which focuses on our call to become like Jesus, the last of all and the servant of all.

THE TWENTY-SIXTH SUNDAY IN ORDINARY TIME

First Reading: Numbers 11:25-29
The Book of Numbers, the fourth book of the Bible, tells the story of the people's wandering in the desert as they journeyed towards the Promised Land. Soon after setting out from Mount Sinai the people complain about the difficulties they are experi-encing and the task of leadership appears to be too much for Moses. He appeals to God for help and God's answer is to share some of the spirit that Moses has with seventy chosen leaders. This event occurs in the Tent of Meeting, the place of the divine

presence in the camp. The cloud indicates God's presence in the tent yet it is clear from what follows that this is not the only way in which God acts. We are told that two others who were not there also received the spirit and began to prophesy. When Joshua, who has been Moses' righthand man discovers what Eldad and Medad are doing he wants Moses to intervene, supposedly to show his authority. Moses, however, gets to the heart of the matter by saying: 'If only the Lord had given his Spirit to everyone in Israel.'

Second Reading: James 5:1-6
We have already noted how direct and forthright James is in putting across his point, and in this reading we have the clearest evidence yet. It should be noted that this is not simply an attack on the rich, as it were out of nowhere. In the preceding verses he has been warning the wealthy against being presumptuous and behaving in a manner which suggested that they were always in control of their own destiny. This is clearly not the case. In a manner typical of the Old Testament prophets, he warns them that they will be held accountable for their actions. In the Day of Judgement their wealth will be of no benefit to them if they have cheated their workers and done nothing to alleviate the sufferings of others.

Gospel: Mark 9:38-43, 47-48
At first glance this collection of sayings do not appear to have a lot in common but in fact everything here is a challenge to those who claim to follow Christ to pay attention to their attitudes and motivation. This is because they have been given an awesome responsibility and they must not presume they are somehow superior to others. Jesus first corrects John for stopping someone doing the work of the kingdom because he is 'not one of us.' There is no on place for elitism among his followers and indeed anyone who shows them a simple kindness will be blessed. This means that there is an onus on the disciples to reflect the work and attitudes of their master. Just as he reached out to the sinners and outcasts so must they – failure to do so will result in harsh judgement because they will be undermining the very project they are called to serve. This is why they must avoid any-

thing that would lead them to sin. The true disciple will be the one who knows how to rejoice in the good that is done by whatever source and who also knows that his or her own behaviour can make it hard for others to come to faith. The lesson here is to examine ourselves and to judge no-one else!

Reflection

Two aspects of what might be called worldly thinking are challenged in the first and second readings. It is often the case that people with power and authority will guard it jealously and exercise it in a way which promotes their status more than it actually serves others. It is this behaviour which is shown to be at odds with what God wants in the Book of Numbers. Joshua has to learn that leadership is about service and Moses as a true leader has the humility to teach him. So too in the Letter of James the worldly view that wealth brings freedom to live our lives exactly as we would like is knocked on the head. We are only travellers and we should always live with an eye to our final destination.

THE TWENTY-SEVENTH SUNDAY IN ORDINARY TIME

First Reading: Genesis 2:18-24

In the book of Genesis the story of creation is presented in two ways. The first in chapter 1 is a poetic account of creation by the word of God which took place over seven days. The second account, from which this reading is taken, tells the story of the creation of humankind. The man comes first but God is aware that he is incomplete, that he should not be alone. The first solution is to create the animal world over which man is given control since he is asked to name the creatures. However, the wonder and beauty of the natural world do not solve the problem of man's loneliness. So God lets the man fall into a deep sleep and from his own substance creates a partner who is right for him. The man responds with his first recorded words, a poem to celebrate this new relationship which gives meaning to his existence. These accounts were not intended to be either scientific or historical; rather they seek to explain God's intention for humanity and the world and they show that married love is at the heart of God's plan. This helps to explain Jesus' rejection of divorce when he is questioned about it in today's gospel.

Second Reading: Hebrews 2:9-11
Although Hebrews is often called a letter, its form is more like that of a sermon. We do not know who wrote it, where it was written or to whom. However, it is safe to say that the author was a person from within the Jewish tradition who had an amazing grasp of the significance of the death and resurrection of Jesus and who wished to convince other Jewish Christians that they should not abandon their new-found faith in Jesus.

In the early part of the work the author seeks to counter a suggestion that Jesus was some form of heavenly being such as an angel. He stresses from the outset that Jesus has a unique dignity and role as the Son of God. He took on our human nature so that he could bring that nature to a new and more intimate relationship with God. It is as our brother who has shared in our sufferings that Jesus is able to lead us to true holiness.

Gospel: Mark 10:2-16
The gospels agree that Jesus, unlike his contemporaries in the Pharisee movement, takes a very strong line on divorce. He argues from God's plan in Genesis (see first reading) that the original intention for marriage was that it should be a covenant of love willed by God and that it should not be set aside by any human agency. This answer no doubt shocked his disciples who would have, like their contemporaries, taken divorce for granted. However, when questioned, Jesus drives the point home forcefully by speaking of adultery and divorce in the same breath and then also of women divorcing. This was not allowed among the Jews but did occur among the Gentiles. So Jesus is calling for a radical rethink on the nature of married love, one that rejects the dominant view based on a husband's power over his wife and instead emphasises the relationship of equals intended by God. This challenging teaching is followed by another exhortation on the appropriate way to receive the kingdom. It is worth remembering that it is not so long since Jesus advised his disciples that anyone who welcomes a child welcomes him. Now we find them preventing the children from coming to him and not sur-

prisingly he is angry with them. This is not just because of the incident but because of their repeated failure to really listen to what he is telling them.

Reflection
The message from the Bible in relation to the sexes is that this relationship is not built on superiority but on complementarity. It is a message that with the passage of time and the rise of patriarchal societies has become blurred. Genesis insists that both are equally made in the image and likeness of God (Gen 1:26-27) and share fully in the destiny which is theirs as children of God. Unfortunately Jesus does not offer specific pastoral advice for people who find themselves in broken marriages but we do know that we are always called to be compassionate as our heavenly Father is compassionate.

THE TWENTY-EIGHTH SUNDAY IN ORDINARY TIME

First Reading: Wisdom 7:7-11
This is the last of the books in the Old Testament and dates from sometime around 60BC. It was probably written for Greek-speaking Jews in Alexandria (Egypt) and presents their faith in a way that would speak to people in a culture which gave pride of place to philosophy. It makes a claim to have been written by King Solomon but this is only to give it the ring of authenticity since Solomon was considered the great wise man of the biblical tradition. In this extract he is extolling the gift of wisdom which he had received in answer to his prayer (1 Kings 3:4-10). In keeping with the themes of wisdom elsewhere in the Bible, it is acknowledged as the most precious treasure, more to be desired than wealth, health and beauty. In the gospel for today Jesus, who is the wisdom of God made flesh, points out to the rich young man that the treasure he owns is keeping him from the true wisdom that Jesus offers.

Second Reading: Hebrews 4:12-13
In the verses preceding this reading we have had a number of quotations from the Old Testament which the author has been using to show how God's plan has been unfolding. Central to

that plan is a willingness to heed the word of God and this is what leads to this very powerful and inspiring piece on the nature of God's word. The first point to be made is that this word is not some kind of dead letter recorded in a book from long ago. Rather it is alive and active. What we read is a reflection of how God has acted in the past and continues to do, right up to the present. This means that he is making himself known to every generation and if we are open then his word goes to the deepest core of our being and elicits a response from us.

Gospel: Mark 10:17-30

The demands of discipleship and the need to deny oneself in order to become a servant or a slave have already been mentioned in this part of Mark's gospel. Now in this story we are presented with a drama that puts flesh on that teaching. A rich man approaches Jesus to ask what must he do to inherit eternal life. He is given the basic answer which requires that he keep the commandments. However, as a practising Jew this is something he would already have known and clearly he is aware that something is still lacking in his life. Jesus senses his hunger and puts a radical challenge to him. He must rid himself of the attachment to wealth, wherein lies his security and social status, and trust himself completely to God by following Jesus. The man becomes sad and the onlookers are shocked as Jesus states that wealth is an obstacle to the true reception of the kingdom. For them wealth was considered a sign of divine favour but Jesus insists that it is a barrier and this is because the ideal of love – the driving force of the kingdom – goes beyond the keeping of commandments and demands that we empty ourselves of our attachments in order to become the servant of others. This is not just for the chosen few but part and parcel of the Christian vocation. Clearly we are not all asked to become St Francis of Assisi but we should be careful not to skip over this passage as though it were not intended for us. The challenge of detachment is one for every follower of Jesus.

Reflection

Since the Second Vatican Council Catholics have been called upon to read and pray the scriptures for, as St Jerome said,

'Ignorance of the scriptures is ignorance of Christ.' Thankfully many have responded to this call and have found their faith life enriched beyond measure and have discovered that the word of God is indeed alive and active. Sadly for many others the Bible is still a closed book. Let us pray for and work towards that day when all Catholics will feel at home taking up their Bible in order to deepen their relationship with the living God.

THE TWENTY-NINTH SUNDAY IN ORDINARY TIME

First Reading: Isaiah 53:10-11

This short reading from Isaiah is taken from the fourth of the so-called 'Servant Songs' which we have already encountered this year (Is 52;13-53:12). This poem celebrates how, through fidelity to his mission even in the midst of suffering and rejection, God's servant brings about the salvation of all. It is important to understand that when the reading says 'God was pleased to crush his servant with suffering', that it is not suggesting that God takes any pleasure in human misery. Quite the contrary, God is anxious to bring about the end of suffering and to that end he allows this faithful person to undergo this experience so that others may be saved. The ideas present in the Servants Songs represent a new direction in Old Testament theology as the prophet seeks to come to terms with that most difficult of questions – the role of suffering in God's plan. After the death and resurrection of Jesus the first generation of believers saw in this text a prophecy of the passion and its saving effects for all people.

Second Reading: Hebrews 4:14-16

The author of this remarkable sermon continues to reflect on Jesus' role in our salvation, this time likening him to the high priest of the Jerusalem temple except this priest has offered the perfect sacrifice, himself. Since he is like us and shares our human condition, he knows what we go through and for this reason we can have great confidence in calling upon him when we are in need of help. Unlike the High Priest in the temple who, once a year, could go through to the holy of holies to offer a sacrifice on the feast of Atonement, Jesus has come permanently into the presence of God and made it possible for us to be with him there.

Gospel: Mark 10:35-45

The story of the apostles James and John continues with the theme of discipleship in this section of Mark. To appreciate what unfolds here it is important to remember that in the two chapters before this Jesus has consistently challenged his disciples with the core values of the kingdom. They are to become like children, like servants; they are to give up all attachments; they are to be willing to take up their cross and follow and all this in the context of three predictions of the passion. So it is with that backdrop that James and John coming looking for special status in Jesus' future glory. The extent of their complete incomprehension is baffling but Jesus shows great patience with them and points out that they will indeed share his future but the glory they seek is not his to give. It would be heartening to think that the other ten were annoyed with James and John for the folly of their question but it might be more realistic to believe their concern was that they might have been upstaged by the other two. So when Jesus gathers them around him it is to tell them once again that in the kingdom of God the exercise of power bears no resemblance to what takes place in the world around them. True greatness lies in service and their model for this is Jesus himself.

Reflection

It is a remarkable fact that in Mark, the first of the gospels, one of the consistent themes is that of the incomprehension of the disciples. Again and again they fail to understand what Jesus is talking about and they are also portrayed as being afraid to ask him. They are presented as somewhat self seeking and dull and at times even Jesus becomes exasperated with them (8:14-21). In choosing to present them this way, perhaps Mark was trying to tell us something: take time to recognise yourselves in this portrait of the disciples. The good news is indeed good but it challenges the values that we take for granted and are very much part and parcel of the world we live in. So when we choose the way of the gospel we should not be surprised that it involves a steep learning curve and we may well turn out to be slow learners!

THE THIRTIETH SUNDAY IN ORDINARY TIME

First Reading: Jeremiah 31:7-9

The Prophet Jeremiah lived at a time of great upheaval on the international stage. As usual Israel was caught up in the midst of events which were way beyond her control. While the Assyrian Empire which had destroyed the north of the country was now in decline, a new power was emerging which would engulf Judea and Jerusalem. Yet it is in these circumstances that Jeremiah has the courage and to speak of how God would save his people. This reading is taken from a section of Jeremiah called the Book of Consolation and it offers hope and encouragement to those who are most vulnerable in times of war and conflict. God will bring home again the lame and the blind, the pregnant women and the mothers with young children. He will do this because he is a father to them all and wishes them to come to no harm. The imagery is tender and full of compassion and speaks movingly of God's saving will for his people.

Second Reading: Hebrews 5:1-6

In this section of the sermon the author of Hebrews is preparing to explain how Jesus is the compassionate high priest sent by God to offer the sacrifice that would take away our sins. To do this he points out a few truths about the high priests who officiated in the temple in Jerusalem. As human beings they were weak and able to sympathise with others. They too were sinners and so had to offer sacrifice for their sins and were called by God to perform this task. God too would call Jesus but while he shared our weakness as a human being, as God's Son he did not sin and so he could offer the perfect sacrifice. This is a new priesthood, not temporal like that of the temple, but rather eternal like that of Melchizedek. He was a priest king who blessed Abraham in Genesis 14 and for the author of Hebrews he plays an important role in his efforts to show how Jesus was a true priest even though he did not belong to the priestly families of Jerusalem.

Gospel: Mark 10:46-52

The story of the healing of Bartimaeus, the blind beggar, brings to a close the section of Mark that began in 8:27 (the twenty-fourth Sunday of the year). As we have seen the focus has been on the meaning and demands of discipleship. Just prior to this incident Jesus has spoken to James and John saying to them, 'What do you want me to do for you?' Now he uses the same words, not to one of his closest companions but to a blind beggar sitting by the road who is crying out to him in desperation. James and John were seeking glory, Bartimaeus just wants to see and to gain that he throws away the only thing he owns, his cloak, lest it impede him in his journey to Jesus. His prayer is granted, he receives perfect sight and his response is to follow Jesus along the way. Jesus is leaving Jericho and heading for Jerusalem and so Bartimaeus is presented to us not simply as a recipient of the healing ministry of Jesus but as the model disciple who begs for sight so that he can follow Jesus to the cross and beyond. In the gospel, sight is often used as a metaphor for faith, being able to see God at work and to follow in the steps of Jesus.

Reflection

These readings are talking about salvation. It is one of those words much used in religious conversation but whose exact meaning is unsure for many. Probably most of us think of salvation as having to do with getting to heaven. However, the prophet Jeremiah only thought of God as saving his people in the here and now, offering them comfort, shade and fresh water. For him these are symbols of salvation. The author of Hebrews by contrast was very aware of heaven but for him salvation came about through the solidarity shown by Jesus who became the way we are so that we might become like him. What comes across strongly in the readings is that God never abandons us and that when we speak of salvation we are speaking of the ways in which God brings us to himself, a process which begins now. Lord, that we may see!

The Thirty-first Sunday in Ordinary Time

First Reading: Deuteronomy 6:2-6

Even though the book of Deuteronomy was probably written sometime in the seventh century BC, it is set in a period some five hundred years earlier when the Israelites, having crossed the wilderness were finally about to enter the Promised Land. Moses, who is soon to die, addresses them and reminds them of all that has happened to them. The book is a calling to mind of the covenant into which they entered on Mount Sinai and in it Moses pleads with the people above all to be faithful. In this lies their future well-being and happiness: being true to the God who freed them from oppression and slavery. In today's text we have what are for the Jewish people the best known verses in the Bible. It is a prayer known as the *Shema*, from the Hebrew word to listen and it is recited twice a day by Jews the world over. It is a call to always remember their God, the one Lord who is Yahweh and to love him above everything else. The Book of Deuteronomy stresses that Israel's relationship with God is to be one of mutual love. God has chosen them out of love and they in turn are to respond with love. This relationship is perfectly embodied in the life of Jesus who in today's gospel recites the *Shema*.

Second Reading: Hebrews 7:23-28

Continuing his comparison between the relationship with God before Jesus and what has now taken place because of Jesus, the author of the Letter to the Hebrews emphasises the flawed nature of the priesthood in the temple. These were mere men, generations of them, who came and went offering sacrifices that failed to bring us any closer to God. Now, however, through Jesus who is risen from the dead and who intercedes for us in heaven all that is changed. We have in him the ideal priest because while he is one of us he has lived perfectly for God, without sin or selfishness. By offering his life he has offered the perfect sacrifice once and for all and now as a result everyone has access to the throne of God.

Gospel: Mark 12:28-34

One of the earliest heresies dealt with by the early church was led by Marcion, a man who taught that the Old Testament had nothing useful to say about God. He affirmed that Jesus presented a new God in his Father. Marcion failed to grasp that the prophetic vision of Jesus was entirely rooted in the scriptures of the chosen people and this is very evident in the scene put before us now. At the heart of Judaism is the *Shema*, the call to love God wholly and completely. The reason for this call was an awareness that Yahweh had revealed himself to his people through the Sinai covenant and, in the events of the exodus, had shown himself as a compassionate saviour. The chosen people where therefore acutely aware that their faith was based on practice and could not be separated from love of neighbour. In the gospel, Jesus and the scribe agree on these essentials and so offer us a reminder of what is also at the core of Christianity.

Reflection

'You shall love the Lord your God with all your heart, with all your soul and with all your strength.' Was this simply the setting of an impossible ideal? For it would seem that much of the history of the People of God is merely a demonstration of how much they failed to live up to their calling. It is as though the priests offering sacrifices in the temple were busy trying in vain to keep open the lines of communication between heaven and earth. Jesus, however, lived out the *Shema* to the very point of laying down his life and in so doing he unblocked the path between God and humanity. This is how he became our way to the Father and changed what seemed like an impossible ideal into a wonderful opportunity. We really can love God because he has loved us first.

THE THIRTY-SECOND SUNDAY IN ORDINARY TIME

First Reading: 1 Kings 17:10-16

The context for this story, which is set during the reign of King Ahab, is a prolonged drought which has devastated the land and which is seen as a punishment on the king for his rejection of the covenant. The prophet Elijah is told to leave the land and his survival is guaranteed by God. While travelling in pagan territory, he comes across a widow who is suffering extreme destitution but in her need she is prepared to share what she has. Her generosity is rewarded and she is provided with food for her son and herself. In the Old Testament the widow is a symbol of those in need, those most at risk. This is because without a man to provide for her she is vulnerable to exploitation. Hence God is concerned for widows and orphans and this is one of the precepts of the covenant. Here the pagan woman's response stands in stark contrast to that of King Ahab whose only interest is in increasing his power and wealth.

Second Reading: Hebrews 9:24-28

In last week's reading from Hebrews the emphasis was on the priesthood; this week the stress falls on the sacrifice being offered. This was the unique insight of the author of this amazing document. Jesus is both perfect priest and perfect sacrifice. To explain this he likens the practice of sacrificing in the temple to an action on earth that seeks to emulate what is going on in heaven. The Holy of Holies in the Jerusalem Temple is a model of the throne of God in heaven. Each year on the Day of Atonement the High Priest enters the Holy of Holies with a sacrifice for the sins of the people. In doing so he is expressing a hope for reconciliation with God and the forgiveness of the people's sins. What has taken place with Jesus is that he, as the compassionate High Priest has truly entered into God's presence bringing with him not the blood of sacrificed animals but his own blood, the gift of his life. Thus the relationship between God and sinful humanity has been restored once and for all.

Gospel: Mark 12:38-44

This incident takes up a theme present in the first reading, namely that those who show the greatest generosity are not always those with the most to give. However, before Jesus comments on the poor widow who gives of her all he roundly condemns those whose behaviour brings the practice of religion into discredit. Their aim is to be noticed and well thought of because of their adherence to religious ritual but by their actions they are revealed as oppressors who care nothing for the plight of those most in need, in fact they even add to their misery. This is a sham that offends Jesus to the core. It is in the context of condemning such behaviour that he notices the poor widow whose actions show her to be a woman of deep faith and trust. It is worth pointing out that Jesus is not suggesting that the poor who give of what they have and leave themselves with nothing are doing what is expected of them. No, he is merely using the behaviour of the woman the show up the inadequacies of others who could learn much from her.

Reflection
In the modern era it is no doubt hard for us to relate to language about the blood of animals and sacrifices by priests in the temple. However, the language of sacrifice is still very relevant to our world. Ironically this can be seen in the first reading where the actions of a poverty-stricken widow show us that the only sacrifice that matters is self sacrifice. God is not interested in the spilling of blood for this makes no change either in him or us. Rather God is concerned about whether we live for ourselves or for others, and Jesus in offering his life, not just by his death on the cross but by everything he did, has shown us the way.

THE THIRTY-THIRD SUNDAY IN ORDINARY TIME

First Reading: Daniel 12:1-13
The Book of Daniel was written at the time of the persecution of the Jews by Antiochus Epiphanes between 167 and 163BC. He was a Greek emperor who was seeking to impose foreign religious practices on the Jews and this led to a revolt by the Maccabee brothers who successfully opposed him. The second part of Daniel (chapters 7-12 in particular) reflects the situation at this time. It is written in the style of an apocalypse, that is to say a revelation. The young Daniel who apparently lives in Babylon during the exile (586-540) receives visions which reveal the path of history and show how God will always triumph over the powers of evil. The events which are predicted in these visions have in fact already taken place and in the reading for today we see how all those who remained faithful during times of persecution are rewarded at the time of the resurrection. This

is the first clear reference to a final judgement and belief in the resurrection in the Old Testament and it is striking that it arose during a time of persecution when people were being martyred for their faith. It is also noteworthy that those who have played a role in instructing the people are given special mention.

Second Reading: Hebrews10:11-14, 18
This reading acts as a summary for all that we have been saying about the letter to the Hebrews, affirming as it does the new situation which now exists because of the death and resurrection of Jesus. It is not known when exactly the letter was written but it may well have happened after the destruction of the Temple in Jerusalem by the Romans in 70AD. For some Jewish Christians this event might have provoked a crisis of faith and made them wonder just how God could be at work in the midst of such a calamity. It is thought they, along with all other Jews, were longing for the restoration of the temple and its sacrifices. The unknown author proceeds to write a sermon to convince them of the need to live for today, acknowledging that what Jesus did has created a whole new understanding of God and the gift of forgiveness. The temple sacrifices could never make us perfect whereas the life of grace won for us by Jesus can do just that.

Gospel: Mark 13:24-32
The last chapter of Mark before the events of the Easter is sometime called a 'little apocalypse'. Aware of their Jewish roots, the first Christians made use of apocalyptic writing to present the victory of Jesus over sin and death. Their belief was that the resurrection had ushered in the last days and that Jesus would return soon. Therefore there was an urgency to their preaching of the gospel and we get a flavour of that from this reading. As we approach the end of another liturgical year, the church invites us to reflect on the fact that we are moving towards an ultimate goal, and that no matter how bad things may get God has triumphed and will triumph again. This type of literature is hard for us to relate to as it seems rather dark and fantastic but it is a literature of hope and that is its perennial value.

Reflection

The people for whom both our readings for today were written were probably spending much time thinking about the future and wondering were was God to be found in the violence and bloodshed that was going on around them. In these communities were two people whose names we do not know who had a vibrant vision of hope and they made it their business to share it with those around them. 'Our God will not fail us so do not give up in the face of hopelessness or despair' was the gist of their message. This is still the heart of the gospel message, so let's ask for the faith to believe it and the courage to share it.

THE FEAST OF OUR LORD JESUS CHRIST, UNIVERSAL KING

First Reading: Daniel 7: 13-14

As outlined above, the second half of Book of Daniel consists of a series of apocalyptic (revelatory) visions that explain the passage of history. In today's reading the boy Daniel has just had a dream in which he has seen the rise and fall of the great empires of the world dating from the Babylonians down to the Romans. The vision in this reading comes after the dream and it speaks of a time when an unnamed figure will arise and on this person God will confer sovereignty over the whole world. In depicting him as a 'son of man' the author simply meant a human being as opposed to an angel or a spiritual being. In the New Testament this title would take on messianic significance as the early church saw in Jesus the fulfilment of this vision. Now the risen Christ sits at the right hand of God and the nations serve him. However, the nature of his kingship and the manner in which it would be obtained are not contained in Daniel's vision. Rather we must go to the gospel for this. Jesus is crowned with thorns and his throne is a cross.

Second Reading: Apocalypse 1:5-8

The Book of the Apocalypse or Revelation is the only writing in the New Testament which bears all the hallmarks of the type of apocalyptic writing we find in Daniel. It too was written as a message of hope to Christians facing persecution. Its author introduces himself as John and he says that his words are from

Jesus Christ who is then described in the words of today's reading. In these few verses a great deal is said and it connects with Old Testament prophecies and the gospel accounts of the death of Jesus. What has been achieved by Jesus is nothing less than the creation of a new people of God. He is the Son of Man of the vision in Daniel but he brought about our salvation, not through military victories and the destruction of empires but rather through his death on the cross. He is the one sent by the eternal God who is the beginning and end of all things. This provides the context for the message of hope in the rest of the book. It is a difficult message to understand, shrouded as it is in symbolism and rooted in the history of the chosen people but it is one which celebrates the joy and hope of the Christian calling perhaps more than any other book in the New Testament.

Gospel: John 18:33-37
For the last gospel of the church's year we return to John and this scene from the trial of Jesus before Pilate. Pilate represents the most powerful empire the world has ever known and lives out of a worldview that is utterly contrary to that espoused by Jesus. For Pilate, kings and kingship mean only one thing: a threat to the established order. For Jesus this is the language of the Bible where God is the shepherd king who looks out for the lost and bandages the wounded. For the worldly governor of Judea this is all a pipe dream; for Jesus it is a vision that will endure long after the Roman Empire has crumbled into the dust. By his death and resurrection Jesus has witnessed to the truth about God and those who search for the truth still listen to his voice.

Reflection
We don't know how many people witnessed the death of Jesus in Jerusalem. We know that some of those who did were delighted to have him out of the way at last. Others were heartbroken at the death of a truly good man and the shattering into pieces of a dream for something better, a new world order in which love and service would triumph over oppression and hatred. The majority probably just went about their business and reflected that really it is wiser just to keep your head down and say noth-

ing. We can be sure that nobody there thought they were witnessing the death of Christ the Universal King. His kind of kingship has to be learned and not in palaces nor in schools of diplomacy but among the poor and needy and those whom the world has forgotten. For our king is the servant of the poor and we only belong to his court when we do likewise.